FOOTPRINTS
IN THE SEA

EXPLORING THE DISAPPEARANCE OF JESUS

ED CHINN

COOL
RIVER
PUB

Cool River Pub
Franklin, TN
www.coolriverpub.net

Cover and text design by Karen Williams [www.intudesign.net]

ISBN 9780615268842

Printed in the United States of America.

Thy way is in the sea,

        and thy paths are in the great waters;

and thy footsteps are not known.

—PSALM 77:19 (DARBY)

Dedication

I've not met anyone in my years on this planet who carried a purer and more fervent devotion to God than Glen and Roberta Roachelle. That intense fidelity to the Lord also led them into a burning love for God's kids.

And, their love for God's family reached out to include mine. They have given much to the Chinns. They have consistently shared their lives, their property and, at times, even their income with us.

So much of what I know, believe, and am came about because of Glen and Roberta. I dedicate all the hours of research and the proverbial "blood, sweat, and tears" which went into the writing of *Footprints in the Sea* to Glen and Roberta Roachelle.

PREFACE

As light moves across land it creates different perceptions of, say, the Grand Canyon, a pond, or a cathedral through stained glass. It all depends on the gradient angle of the light (time of day) and ingredients in the atmosphere.

I think that is the primary difference (and dissonance) between generations; things just look different from your own location and time of day. I often think of how beautiful it would be if everyone could simply describe what they see from their particular location or time without becoming so identified with it or defensive of it. We would all be richer if everyone helped us to see from their perspective and did so without condescension, dispute, or derogation of other views.

Freely and gratefully do I admit that I have been taught by giants. People like my parents and my grandparents, too many teachers and writers to list, and a host of friends and advisors have shaped my mind and spirit. Like Tennyson, "I am part of all I have seen."[1]

So, to all of the giants in my life, I say that I've tried to simply describe what I see from a particular location or time without contrasting it with what you and others saw from a particular vantage point and at your time of day.

I take immeasurable comfort and guidance from what you saw and continue to see. I will never forget it. Admittedly, the great

---

[1] I've tried to be meticulous in giving attribution to all sources. But, I also know that much of what I've seen has become so much a part of me that I may have forgotten an original source. So, if I've borrowed anything without acknowledgement, I assure you it was unintentional. Please let me know and I'll do all I can to make it right.

landscapes of life and truth may appear slightly different to me. I only hope that what I see is an extension and even a confirmation of the possibilities you visualized and considered.

Thank You

Writing a book is one of the most humbling ventures imaginable.

I worked very hard to write this thing, but then others came roaring in like lions. They read multiple manuscripts, contacted agents and publishing companies, encouraged me when I was weary, corrected me when I was cranky, and even provided underwriting dollars to get the project completed and into print.

How can one ever maintain any dignity after that?

Anyway, I must thank some folks who endured so much to help me get to the finish line.

First, I thank Joanne. We've now been married more than forty years. And, she is the best friend and best critic I've ever known. She read every word of this about forty times. This book is much better than it would have been without her.

The Chinn family could not have been more supportive. After my Dad's mind began slipping away, one day I sat with him, reflecting about the meandering course of my life. Suddenly, he slammed his palm down on their dining room table; his voice boomed, "You're a writer!" It was like God spoke. That statement is a pillar in my life.

Dad is gone now. But, my Mom and my brothers, Vernon and Carl, have reflected Dad's support in so many ways. And, my children—Eddie, Paul, and Amy and their spouses—have also provided consistent help and encouragement.

I also thank Mike and Pam Bishop, John Boaz, Dave and Jen Brukiewa, Rosanne Cash, John Eames, Justin and Valerie Ensor, Darrell Harris, Billy Harrison, Jason Hood, Randy Hood, Patrick

Judd, Brian McLaren, Rex Miller, Stan Moser, Glen and Roberta Roachelle, Lynn Scarborough, Dale Smith, John and Linda Scherrer, Tom Sutter, Chip Watkins, and Karen Williams.

All of you pulled me over the finish line. I will always be grateful.

CONTENTS

INTRODUCTION

I was born into a genuinely devout Christian home. My parents loved me and my brothers, but they loved God more.

Jack and Mary Chinn took the local church very seriously. I grew up watching my Dad and Mom's love of God flow out into deep and graceful service in the church. They filled teaching and other ministry roles. And, Dad fixed the roof, cleaned the carpets, replaced hot water heaters and HVACs, and mowed the lawn. He made sure church doors stayed open and that pastors were paid and had food on the table.

He did it all at his own expense. I have lived in the enormous shadow of his example.

It is also true that the most thrilling adventures of my life have been in local churches. In fact, I was caught in an historic visitation—one of those quivering moments scattered throughout history when God steps into human events, cuts across lives, disrupts patterns and plans, and rewires the genetic material.

I am forever changed because of that visitation to a local church. That soaring connection with the reality of God and the resulting exploits with his kids are the defining experiences of my life. Those days and people and divine moments will forever burn in my memory. Unless I am killed by a wild bullet or buffalo, I suspect my deathbed thoughts will pass again and again over those halcyon days.

In fact, I've been completely and joyfully immersed in the church for most of my life.

And, now, another truth: I have not participated in local church life since 1995.

My leaving was not a rejection of God or of the church. The same faith and love that led me into local church life led me out. In fact, my yearning for God was more vibrant and active when I left the church.

So, why did I leave?

The short version of the story is this: my quest for more of God simply led me to a point where the road had washed out. From there, I had to hike off on my own. Now, I've lived out here in the wilds of faith so long that I no longer miss the church civilization. At last, I find that I'm a spiritual outdoorsman. I love the clear mountain mornings of walking with God. I have no plans to return to the urban congestion of "Christianity."

For several years, I assumed that my situation was unique. Then, over time, I began to notice that more of my friends and acquaintances were drifting away from local church membership. It seemed as though the current to some religious electromagnet had been turned off and the formerly galvanized particles were floating away. Today, very few of my friends remain active in traditional patterns of church life. Still, I didn't give it much thought; I wasn't particularly interested in other people's church habits or attitudes. I was primarily focused on my own walk.

Then a larger landscape of American church life began crowding into my peripheral vision as I discovered other voices. For example, George Barna says that a genuine and historic "revolution" is reshaping the whole milieu of the church in America. In fact, he calls it "the most significant transition you or I will experience during our lifetime."

So, what is that revolution? According to Barna, "Millions of devout followers of Jesus Christ are repudiating tepid systems and practices of the Christian faith and introducing a wholesale shift in how faith is understood, integrated, and influencing the world."[2] He also sees that, for millions of people caught in this shift, "the local church is nowhere to be found on their agenda."[3] Barna's research shows that more than 20 million people are now part of this realignment and that by the year 2025, only 30-35% of Christians will remain in local churches (as we presently understand that term).[4]

I started writing this book as a purely personal thing. It was born on the twin tracks of devotion and inquiry—devotion to the Lord and inquiry into my own place in his universe. I never expected that anyone else would ever read it. Then, the emerging and surprising awareness that "millions" may be caught in the same shift caused me to see beyond myself.

I slowly began to realize that others may benefit from my search. I hope you are one of them. But, I also suspect that many will not like what I see. Of course, in some cases those who don't like it will still benefit from it ("The truth that sets you free will first make you mad").

And, here is what I see.

I think Barna is accurate in his discovery of a large social phenomenon, but I also think the basic reason behind it may be larger and simpler than his book reveals.

Jesus has disappeared. He is gone. Vanished. No, he hasn't broken the "I-will-never-leave-you-nor-forsake-you" promise. But, he has disappeared from the systems, structures, and expectations we have constructed "for him."

That vast "Christian complex" was built, furnished, and staffed for a myriad of reasons. Some were noble, some were not. But, the

---

[2] George Barna, *Revolution* (Wheaton, IL: Tyndale House Publishers, Inc., 2005) p. 11
[3] Ibid., p. 61
[4] Ibid., p. 49

primary factor driving that construction has been our continual and relentless underestimation of him.

In the interest of full disclosure with you, let me be clear about my own view of the central character of this book. I see Jesus as the purest, wisest, most compassionate, most frightening, most magnificent, and most influential One who ever walked the surface of this planet. He is the Son of God and was born on earth of a virgin. He remained here for thirty-three years on a royal and official "state visit" from Heaven. When that visit ended, he was executed, was buried, and rose from death. By his resurrection, he conquered death. He is the King and he reigns forever over all created order.

He makes all things new.

You should also know that I love local churches and those who lead and serve them. My respect for pastors and other church leaders is almost unbounded.

Although some will read this book as criticism of the local church, that is not at all what has driven my writing. My real purpose is to gaze at the God Who is Larger. From that gaze, I conclude that many local churches are trying much too hard to help. The best and healthiest thing for local churches is to get the roles straight: God's and the churches.' If he is really God, then humans everywhere can take a deep sigh and settle into the billowing and bottomless depths of his love and kindness.

My purposes in writing this book are:

1. *To recognize* convulsions and collapses of the old forms of the church.
2. *To remind* all of us that the Lord is larger than, pre-existent to, and distinct from the church
3. *To rekindle* devotion to him and passion for his kingdom.

4. *To release* people to confidently explore the new pathways of walking with God.

Finally, while it was a washed-out road which led me into the wild, I do not assume that all roads have washed out. Nor do I think that everyone should live out where I do.

I freely admit that many are very happy in their local church. And, many local churches continue to be touchpoints between Heaven and earth. Because they are so God-focused, they really do display "the manifold wisdom of God" in the earth (Ephesians 3:10).

I'm not on a crusade against the institutional church at all. I sincerely hope this book will not be interpreted as "anti-church." I personally think of what I'm saying is post-church or, in some senses, pre-church. I am not a "prophetic voice." Rather, I am just trying to address an attitude which blinds people—religious, pagan, or bored—to the reality, largeness, and generosity of God.

Despite the wonderful examples to the contrary, that attitude has in fact flourished in the modern American church. That's why millions are leaving. They must leave, in order to find the Lord.

To all who take offense at anything in these pages, I offer my sincere apology. I mean no insult or injury. If anyone is offended or feels wounded, I invite you to follow Jesus' own directive for resolving disputes:

> *If a fellow believer hurts you, go and tell him — work it out*
> *between the two of you. If he listens, you've made a friend.*
> (MATTHEW 18:15, THE MESSAGE)

I'll do my best to listen and be your friend.

ED CHINN, FORT WORTH, TEXAS
JANUARY 3, 2009

Chapter 1

THE WRONG QUESTION

The great American story is told very well in the Apollo 13 saga. Spaceship in trouble, the courage to face that problem, and then the old-fashioned mix of American confidence, ingenuity, and technology which fixes it. It's a great epic of our folk religion and most of us know it, love it, and live it; if there's a problem, we can solve it.

That American characteristic has naturally seeped into our approach to God.

So, when I talk about the problems of the church in America, the first question is the predictable and oh-so-American: "What do we do about this?"

It is precisely the wrong question. It flows from an attitude rooted in our American mind, not the Bible. The question assumes our own power and competence. And, part of the problem is that we have relied on our own power and competence. We assume we can analyze it, plan it, do it, fix it. No problem.

I think that is why American Christianity seems obsessed with "how to do church." Programs, websites, books, tape series, seminars, and conferences dedicated to rethinking and reworking church are thriving everywhere. Everyone—denominational, traditional, seeker, postmodern, emergent, whatever—seems to sense that "we gotta do something." Besides launching an enormous jobs program, this hammering sense of urgency exaggerates our own prominence and power. It also verifies our silent acceptance that Jesus has disappeared. We instinctively know we're the only ones left here. Anybody got any ideas? Let's try 'em.

Several years ago, I attended a reception given in honor of a distinguished and famous Christian writer. Although he was highly accomplished and quite venerable, he did not have a gregarious personality. He was not a commanding figure; the room didn't revolve around him. Rather, he was very quiet and gracious.

I was the sixth person to arrive. The writer was already seated in one corner of the large, well-furnished, living room. Two other people and the host couple were sitting together in the corner farthest from this revered man. Incredibly, no one was talking to or even seated near him. I quickly pulled a chair close to the writer and began engaging him. It took some work, but after a while, he began to open up. I discovered a true and delightful treasure.

As others arrived, they noticed him, spoke or nodded a greeting, paused in awkward silences, and then quickly gravitated toward the other, more boisterous and entertaining, end of the large living room.

At one point, even though I was not the host, I clinked a fork to a crystal glass and gathered everyone's attention. After trying to build a proper platform for him, I asked the writer if he could share a particular story that he had told in one of his books. He spoke softly and timidly as he began the tale. Within one minute, those polarized to the other end of the room resumed their conversation with each other, ignoring him altogether. He clumsily turned his attention to me, forced to address the only one who was still listening. He and I both were embarrassed.[5]

---

[5] Later, I learned that his host planned to send him to the airport in a cab! Of course, I quickly

I have often thought back on that scene as a picture of the way Christians tend to relate to God. He is the professed and official reason we gather. Yet, because he speaks in the "still, small voice," we are pulled toward the louder voices, the brighter swirling colors, the more frenzied activities.

The mind and heart of the Lord are open to those who seek him. But, it takes time and work to seek God—he is not sensual or gregarious. He is not the life of the party. As Spirit, He does not make it easy for our sensual approach to life. It is much easier and faster to relate to the sounds and sights which are peripheral to him.

In fact, modern church life tends to exist completely independent of him. The writer of my reminiscence could have walked out of the room, climbed into a car, and driven into a lake; no one would have noticed and the party would have continued. How can the Lord be "lifted up" in our midst if we are not entirely in a waiting posture? It seems logical to assume that one who is truly waiting doesn't do anything unless and until the person, event, or idea being waited for appears. Isn't that the lesson of Saul's decision (in I Samuel 13) to go ahead and "do church" even though God's representative (Samuel) wasn't there? I can only conclude that, like Saul, our church life owes its existence to other factors and forces. Our "waiting on the Lord" only lasts until other conforming pressures becomes too strong.

I often wonder if, when I claim to seek him, I'm only seeking him within the confines of my predetermined religious assumptions and boundaries. Some are designed (perhaps subconsciously) to keep intimacy away. I have to be honest; He scares me. So, I place certain protective embankments around my "quiet time."

Is "quiet time" itself an idea which tries to build a wall of

---

volunteered to drive him. I will always treasure that one hour ride spent with the author.

protection. Could it be my rebellious heart serving notice on God that he really needs to observe my rules of engagement, my own parameters for this meeting? *Don't get loud or violent with me, God!* Would Job understand "QT?" Read about his "devotional time" (Job 38–42); here was a man trapped in a box canyon with a tornado and a keg of nails. It is probably the most shredding God-man conversation ever recorded.

That's why I've had to face the fact that I'm not really seeking after him. I'm seeking my own contrived, preferred, and harmless notions of him. To honestly seek him means I might get him.

To seek God is to throw every other consideration, comfort, and concept out the window. It assumes nothing and demands nothing. A purity of seeking the Lord is a unique mix of patience and restlessness, waiting and pressing, fear and confidence, respect and risk. I think that kind of heart is probably content to find him in a blizzard, a bar, a mortuary, a movie, a roadhouse, a novel, on a mountain, in the depths of the sea, or . . . in a building we call "church."

Frankly, I think there may be too much community implied in the "what should we do" question. Do healthy communities produce healthy individuals? To a degree, yes. But, individuals must be brought to some level of maturity in the furnace of God's "severe mercy" before they can function and flow in community. So, perhaps he is stripping us back to "no one in here but you and me." Maybe, like Abraham, like Moses, like Peter, I have to deal with him as an individual before I'm fit for community.

STOP!

I like Eugene Peterson's translation of Romans 12:2 in The Message: "Don't become so well-adjusted to your culture that you fit into it without even thinking. Instead, fix your attention on God . . ."

We all tend to live on unthinking autopilot. For example, when we think of Christian life, we assume that it must include things like "attending" church, having a "worship experience," telling others about Jesus, becoming politically active, listening to Christian radio, reading Christian books, opposing (or supporting) abortion and gay marriage, etc. Any of those ideas or activities may be right. But, when we just *assume* they are right, they take on a life and substance of their own. In time, they become the center and sum of our faith. We end up "so well-adjusted to our culture that we fit into it without even thinking." When that happens, God is irrelevant. We do what we do because of the cultural constraints.

So, how do we "fix our attention on God?" To really do that requires that we come to him without any assumptions at all.

Doing that usually requires us to just STOP! Everything. Psalms 46:10 carries the admonition to "cease striving and know that I am God." (NAS). Again, Eugene Peterson's *The Message* brings it to life: "Step out of the traffic! Take a long, loving look at me, your High God, above politics, above everything."

In other words, how can he be the leader if our cultural assumptions have a momentum of their own? Followers follow. To follow requires that we forget what we think we know and wait for leader initiative.

I think following him requires an elegant ignorance.

In 1995, my wife Joanne and I left the high-pressure intensity of Washington, DC and moved to a 30-acre farm in rural Tennessee. We did, indeed, "step out of the traffic and took a long, loving look at God, above politics, above everything." For almost a year, we did not attend a church service. I locked the gate to the property, sat in a rocking chair on the front porch, watched the deer play, smoked a few cigars, drank superb medicinal liquids from Scotland, and talked to God. It was like fasting. Crud fell away, clarity returned, we found a new pace of life that we maintain to this day.

We became elegantly ignorant; we allowed the Lord to over-haul and renovate our faith. It was one of the healthiest and most beneficial periods of our life.

Why are we so focused on Church?

For most of his working life, my Dad was a railroad brakeman. In addition, he also served the church; bought, built and remod-eled homes; managed oil investments; wrote columns for the Pratt (Kansas) Daily Tribune; served on the board of the local museum; and did some farming.

I often came home from school, walked in the house, and yelled, "Where's Dad?" Sometimes Mom would say, "He's down at the farm" or "he left on the railroad" or other information about Dad's location. At that point, if I wanted to see him, I knew I'd have to go where he was. There was nothing strange in that; Dad had lots of work to do. His absence didn't set up panic. Besides, even when he was gone, Jack Chinn was still everywhere in the house and all over our property. Dad filled us and our whole world. Everything we did when he was gone was the same as if he were standing right there (except for the normal—and short-lived—boyhood rebellions).

When Dad was home, we lived in response to him. Dad was the metronome; his "beat" set our work and play and worship rhythms. Our dinner times were often long and relaxed and fun. Life didn't clatter and jump all around him. Mom didn't run up and down the hallway in frantic performance of her "wife" pro-gram. Vernon, Carl, and I did not gyrate and bounce around the yard in our *Chinnian* activities.

When Dad was away, Mom didn't panic and try to figure out a new way to "do" marriage and family. She didn't talk to the neighbors to see what other family models existed on our street …

"Hmmm, I wonder if what the Stiversons are doing could work here."

Obviously, it would have been unnatural and just plain weird to try to "do Chinn." We were and are Chinns. It would have been even more aberrant to consider our house or our dining table as synonyms for our family. It certainly never occurred to us to erect a sign in our front yard announcing "House of Chinn."

One of the ironies of the visible church—ostensibly the "Body of Christ—is that, in the words of my friend Charles Simpson, it "does every Sunday what Jesus never did any Sunday."[6]

How did that kind of contradictory pattern ever develop?

Eagles and Beetles

Many years ago, I read an obscure account by a British authority on eagles. In telling his story, the old scientist revealed that he had spent the first half of his life in the study of beetles. Then, one summer he retreated to his cabin, high in the mountains of Scotland, to work on his beetle collection (he didn't explain and only God knows how one does that). And there, on a lazy summer afternoon, he spread his glass cases of beetle specimens on tables and sawhorses in a grassy clearing near his cabin.

As he bent over to work on a particular display, puffing his pipe, an eagle came swooping out of the sky and screamed; its enormous shadow darkened his field of sight and severely frightened him. In the calamitous moment, he looked up at the majestic wingspan and knocked his glass case of beetles to the ground and broke it. Beetles popped out of their spaces. The wind scattered them.

He wrote, "I never looked down again." He devoted the rest of his life to eagles.

---

[6] Of course, Jewish religion assumed regular participation in temple life. But, the modern programmatic, activity-driven, consumerist pattern of church life does not resemble anything Jesus ever did or endorsed.

Of course, it is a problem that we remain obsessed with small specimens and microscopic views. But, I wonder if the larger problem is that we've never seen the eagle.

That is why I'd rather staple my tongue to a tree than to attend most Christian conferences. It's like listening to dry prosaic lectures on beetles, the exhibit halls or trade show components are like glass cases of insect specimens, and the music is often attended by the odor of formaldehyde.

I often wonder what would happen if Jesus, the Eagle, came swooping into one of these God-forsaken events.

I tend to live out the lie that the same human cleverness that created the problem can now solve it. I can so easily assume that I and others understand the gravity of the situation in ways he doesn't. And, that leads me to believing that we're the ones who can fix it. But, sometimes, we can't fix it. We can only wait for him. After all, it's his church, not ours.

In 1988, columnist and TV personality Cal Thomas was asked in my presence what he thought of the "Washington for Jesus" rally. Cal replied that he didn't go. Then, he added that he felt bad about it and tried to repent. "But, the Lord said, 'Oh, Cal, don't worry about it; I didn't go either.'"

Now, of course, I know that Jesus was there. But, I do think Thomas' irreverent humor reflects God's attitude about "going to church" in America today; He doesn't go either!

I do not attend a regular church service. In fact, I am not doing anything but seeking him. Jesus is the Author, Designer, Builder, Shepherd, King. I'm only searching for him; *where* he is staying or speaking is unimportant to me. And, I'd rather have him, in a time and place of his choosing, than to live with a fabrication of something just because it looks "scriptural" or is considered a cultural requirement. I just want to be near him.

So, what about church attendance?

The real issue, of course, is not in whether people attend or don't attend regular meetings of the church in a local area. That is a personal decision.

However, the church is a relational, familial reality; it is not a meeting. The idea of "attending family" is absurd. We are family at breakfast, in the car, walking through a forest, huddled in the emergency room, standing at the grave. Family is not a meeting. Neither is church.

We *are* church; we don't *do* or "go to" church.

People often use Hebrews 10:25—"not forsaking the assembling of ourselves together"—to make the case that "going to church" is commanded. However, Bible commentator Albert Barnes wrote that the Greek word translated "assembling together" simply means "an act of assembling, or a gathering together." Furthermore, he writes that the word "is nowhere used in the New Testament in the sense of *an assembly or the church*" (italics mine).[7] In other words, that passage is not referring to an official or regular meeting.

According to Adam Clarke, the issue addressed in 10:25 was *fear*, a fear of persecution.[8] Clearly, the recipients of the letter had been through much intimidation, including incarceration and the confiscation of their property (10: 32-34). The author seems to be encouraging them to keep getting together despite that intimidating power of the state. But, this verse is certainly not making the case for regular time and place meetings.

---

[7] Albert Barnes, *Notes on the New Testament* (Grand Rapids, MI: Baker Book House, 1981) p. 237-238
[8] Adam Clarke, *Clarke's Commentary on the Bible, Volume VI* (New York, Abington Press) p. 757

Of course, there are reasons to gather with other Christ-followers in time and space; we tend to die or go nuts when we're isolated from one another. I'm in full agreement that collective worship, group instruction, sharing the Eucharist, congregating around baptisms, and a life exchanging communal reality are vital components of walking with God. But, they should flow out of relational reality. In other words, it seems to me that for those activities and purposes to have meaning, three things are essential:

1. That those gathered have a proper attitude and conduct toward God.
2. That they be purposeful in their gathering.
3. That they have some degree of relationship with, or at least respect for, the others assembled there.

Walter Brueggemann explains one reason to gather in a *regular meeting* of the local church:

> "The church on Sunday morning, or whenever it engages in its odd speech, may be the last place left in our society for imaginative speech that permits people to enter into new worlds of faith . . . There is then a wistful wonderment when we gather again around the text on Sunday morning. What is that text into which I have been baptized? Is there a life carried in the text? Is there indeed a word from the Lord that would let me live?" [9]

I agree. I hunger for that "wistful wonderment;" I ache for "a word from the Lord that would let me live." But, that is now part of the reason I don't attend a regular meeting of a local church. The place Brueggemann describes is too rare in our consumer-driven life. And, I'm weary of trying to find that "imaginative speech" in contemporary church culture. I'm sick of alliteration that

[9] Walter Brueggemann, Finally Comes the Poet (Minneapolis, MN: Augsburg Fortress Press, 1989) p. 3, 8

Footprints in the Sea

has no substance, homilies about self image, and product-based sermons (I once passed three church signs *within one mile* promoting "Purpose-Driven" messages).

The primary reason I ever attend a church service is the hope that I will hear something proclaimed out of heaven, something that carries the majesty, the revelation, the heart and breath of God. I want my heart to burn with a word from Heaven. I want to hear something which rumbles through the corridors of his chamber and then delivers a sonic boom when it enters my earth space. I am not interested in a 3-point guide for living or recycled Oprah or political perspectives or a Bible study or exploring styles of worship. And, frankly, I'm not even looking for more apologetics and theologies.

I want the *sound of Heaven* to invade my heart, scare the hell out of me, and split me wide open. I want my "Edness" to spill out on the ground and for him to take up residence in the suddenly empty (and scared spitless) vessel.

So, what about hell?

I often discuss or speak on the issues surrounding the reality of living as a representative of Heaven on earth. And, so often, those discussions raise the issue of hell. While it may seem tangential to some, I am becoming convinced that our *ideas* about hell are blockades to our ability to think and live biblically.

I am continually astonished that so much of the energy of modern evangelicalism is derived from the idea of hell. As the prime driver of evangelism, "hell" reveals that Christians have a fundamental distrust of God's justice. We cannot bear the thought of humans having to actually face and deal with their Creator and Father. So, we try to mobilize Christians in a global effort to reach everyone who hasn't spoken the specific incantation of a "sinner's prayer" or some other formulaic script which will provide legal protection from his judgment.

I don't dispute the existence of hell. But, I believe the ideas of hell—especially those spawned in nineteenth century evangelism—are distractions away from the reality of the kingdom of God. It has devolved into a way of designing and reinforcing an invented (and self-serving) moral order: heaven for me and mine; hell for those guys. Hell also places the focus on individuals rather than the King; it devalues the idea of salvation, reducing it to some kind of personal fire-insurance. And, that focus creates an illusion that life swirls around me rather than him.

Brian McLaren recalls Jonathan Edwards' famous nineteenth-century sermon, "Sinners in the Hands of an Angry God." Edwards wrote and preached:

> "The God that holds you over the pit of hell, much as one holds a spider or some loathsome insect over a fire, abhors you and is dreadfully provoked; his wrath toward you burns like fire; he looks upon you as worthy of nothing else, but to be cast into the fire."

From that rather severe focal point of religious history, McLaren then goes on to write,

> "...the conventional doctrine of hell has too often engendered a view of a deity who suffers from borderline personality disorder or some worse sociopathic diagnosis. *God loves you and has a wonderful plan for your life, and if you don't love God back and cooperate with God's plans in exactly the prescribed way, God will torture you with unimaginable abuse, forever* . . . [10]

---

[10] Brian D. McLaren, *The Last Word and the Word After That* (San Francisco: Jossey-Bass, 2005) p. xii

Clearly, the most prevalent ideas of hell fail to represent God and his magnificent Spirit and purpose. In fact, I think Hell has very little, if anything, to do with the Kingdom of God.

In the Ghetto

As a church consultant, I have come to believe that a primary reason Christians are so focused on church is, simply, that church and Christian culture represent familiar territory. It is a ghetto in the midst of a world that is alien and intimidating. So, as much as many of us say we want to get out into the real world, we keep finding cloverleaf ramps which curl right back to our little cultural enclave.

Therefore, instead of asking real life questions—like, "What can I do for the community?" "How can I be a better [husband, father, son, mother, neighbor, etc.]?" "Where would the Lord of the whole earth have me go?"—we seem to be more comfortable hanging out in arcane church polity and philosophy issues. We understand the language, we know the other people in the room, and we have a fear of the failure that could happen in the real world.

Of course, that was the same issue that kept the first century Christians in Jerusalem. The Diaspora (and obedience to Jesus' word to "go into all the earth") only happened because death and destruction came to town.

Chapter 2

RAIN

I was born dead.

1:00 p.m., November 8, 1946, in Pratt, Kansas. Thirty-nine hours earlier, the young Mary Chinn was rushed to the hospital with severe uremia and a raging fever. Doctor Cyril Black told her husband Jack that the baby, their first, was surely dead and that Mary may not survive.

And, just as he predicted, I was indeed dead. The doctor quickly tossed me aside in order to save my mother's life. According to reliable witnesses, I was twenty minutes without breath (this may explain much about me). One attending nurse said that "something kept telling me to work with that baby." She did, even though Doctor Black at least once ordered her to "leave that dead baby alone and help me with Mrs. Chinn."

A little while later, out in the waiting room, Dad heard a baby's cry. Knowing that his son was dead, he assumed another baby had just been born. No one has ever offered a clear explanation for how I, reportedly dead for twenty minutes, came back to life.

For much of my life, the first line of Ephesians 2:1 has carried a deep resonance for me. "As for you, you were dead . . ." (NIV) I've always known that I didn't start out with a great bargaining position. I earned or deserved nothing; everything I've encountered, touched, or received has been by the kindness and generosity of God.

Because of the circumstances of my birth, I grew up with a powerful awareness of my own placement in context, limitations, and destiny.

For example, on October 24, 1944, the American aircraft carrier, *USS Princeton*, was bombed and sunk at the Battle of Leyte Gulf. My Dad was one of the survivors. From as early as I can remember, October 24 was almost as large as Thanksgiving in our house. I was always aware that not only Dad's life was saved that day, but also those of three sons. We were all in the water that day. That day was Passover to some Kansas Protestants; the angel of death passed over. That is why "this night is unlike any other night."

That awareness extended to other realities of my life: I did not choose to be born in Kansas. I didn't select Jack and Mary Chinn as my parents or Vernon and Carl to be my brothers. And, I surely don't remember angels giving me a pre-birth check list from which I picked "Pentecostal Fundamentalism." Those choices were made for me (and I am deeply grateful for all of them).

Because of gravity, we are all literally pulled into an inextricable relationship to the land, a primal connection which quickly plunges below the surface of the soil into one of life's deep mysteries. Some places will always carry an ancient hum of ancestral melodies. The topographical features where we live in our formative years—the barn, that stretch of beach, Grandpa's shop, that little playground at the apartment—have a way of forming a sacred geography of the heart.

Stephen Ambrose understood that; he opened his epic saga of Lewis and Clark's Western expedition with this line: "From the west-facing window of the room in which Meriwether Lewis was born on August 18, 1774, one could look out at Rockfish Gap, in the Blue Ridge Mountains, an opening to the West that invited exploration."[11]

---

[11] Stephen Ambrose, *Undaunted Courage* (New York: Touchstone, Simon & Schuster, 1996) p. 19

For example, my own earthwomb, Pratt County, Kansas, is a latticework of section roads engraved across America's heartland prairie. Exactly one mile apart and running perfectly north and south, east and west, that grid contains 1261 miles of dirt roads. As a teenager, I had a summer job of mowing the sides of those roads. Day after day, summer after summer, I crisscrossed the county on a John Deere tractor and mower rig.

Is it merely coincidence that today I tend to see all of life on a crisscrossing framework of straight-line issues, relationships, and propositions? Would my mental software be different if I had been born in Brooklyn or raised in the Rockies? Is geography destiny?

Pratt was an island, a tight bouquet of trees and grain elevators and church steeples rising out of an immense flat sea of prairie grass and farms. And, just as the ocean produces gamblers, the farm country was home to some tough people who constantly risked their lives so that they could strike a working partnership with the earth. To make it work, the weather would have to do its part in pulling a good crop from the ground and the grain and live-stock sale prices would have to rise up to meet them with favor.

Like the sea, farming pulled men and women close to brush their ear with promises and, very often, to cripple or kill them. By the time many farmers make it into their soft satin caskets, their folded and battered hands have lost a couple fingers. Almost every farm family has been touched by variations of the same dry mouth, trembling voice phone call: "Daddy's had an accident." The South Central Kansas of my youth was a generous land, a place of large and sturdy homes, weathered barns, and tractor widows.

It was not "Field of Dreams."

Agricultural life convinced people to throw steel blades into the soil, struggle with banks and merchants, and call on the mercy of God in order to pull daily bread (and maybe an estate) out of the ground. Farmers would buy the equipment, turn the ground, and drill seeds. But if it didn't rain, all the invested labor and money would start blowing away like top soil did in the dust storms of the 1930s.

For a farmer, the scent of rain was the kiss of God. I wonder if that's why the farmers of my childhood were inevitably religious. And, did the advent of irrigation cool the religious impulses which were once so prevalent in agricultural communities and states?

Naturally, with such a heritage and culture, I grew up with a deep sense of God. Kansas is one of those "big sky" areas of the world; Yahweh and Sky formed a seamless transcendence for me. To this day, I study the sky the way some people analyze horoscopes or the stock market. I'm haunted by weather . . . and God.

I think that's why rain has become the Grand Metaphor for me. It forms mysteriously *up* there out of unseen forces and matter. Then, it arrives in wet and powerful force *down here*. We can't control it and we can't live without it and sometimes we cannot live with it. When rain enters our world, it cleanses, nourishes, and often destroys and kills.

It doesn't take very long for that awareness to become a sense of God. Looking up is a natural posture for farmers.

My Dad was the tap root of my identity. Like so many of his generation, he was damaged by that sudden collapse of crop and cattle prices that destroyed many farmers in the 1930s. The Depression pulled a gun on America's farmers and merchants and demanded all they had. Those who lived through it were sure it could happen again. They lived in fear of that thief.

I think Dad was terrorized by the possibility that the thief could, without warning, step out of the shadows of another night.

To him (and Mom), three rapidly growing boys in need of jeans, tooth fillings, and pencils became a new incarnation of the thief. So whenever Dad sensed his presence in our home, he stood trembling, face to face with him, and shouted, "If you'd just think before you write, you wouldn't wear out the erasers so fast," or, "Quit buying them candy. It's rotting every tooth in their head," or "How can he outgrow jeans in a *month*?" Although Dad often appeared to be an angry man, he was probably more fearful than furious.

The most bracing and defining experience of his life was World War II. Surviving the sinking of the *Princeton* pushed this farm kid beyond his physical, emotional, and spiritual borders. All that I ever knew of Jack Chinn had already been mashed through that crucible of fire, water, and death.

To his three little boys Dad was often a warrior with no war. We loved him, he was the finest man we ever knew, and we were terrified of him. Like many World War II vets, Dad brought the war home. The Japanese had been whipped; the next battle ground was the hearts and minds of his sons. Vernon, Carl, and I quickly learned to surrender or suffer. Of course, we projected that attitude on God.

As a Rock Island railroad brakeman, Dad's "office" was a caboose rocking along the tracks, grimy and reeking of the pungent fumes of diesel, oil, and working man sweat. The work could be brutal; hanging from the rear of a train in bone-chilling Kansas blizzards or the suffocating August heat; placing his life in the hands of drunk and deranged engineers; the backbreaking work of wrestling box cars around switching yards; and suffering the indignities of belligerent and blundering co-workers was a tough way for a fine man to make a living. And, like his war, Dad brought his job home also. Hearing the distant mournful whistle of a train was too often a fearful sound to me.

John Goldsberry, my maternal grandfather, was a Missouri moonshiner. Hard times pushed him into this supplemental and very clandestine career. He not only made and sold the stuff, but he also drank quite a bit of it. His daughter Mildred remembers him crawling around on the floor crying because he'd gone (temporarily) blind from drinking bad stuff. Evidently, he didn't utilize FDA standards in maintaining the purity of his product.

In 1936, he was employed as part of a road gang, building blacktops around Buffalo, Missouri. One warm spring evening he stood with other workers by the side of the road, listening to the road foreman give instructions about the next day's work. Across the road and about a hundred yards away, gospel singing flowed out the open windows of a Pentecostal church. Gradually, as it became darker, Grandpa slipped away from the foreman's meeting and made his way down the road to the church house. He crouched beneath a window and listened to the stirring and beautiful songs. The next morning, his kids awoke to their Daddy singing the songs he heard as he squatted in the darkness.

That marked the beginning of Pentecostalism's pull on the Goldsberry family. One year later, they all fled Missouri in the middle of the night (the real and complete story remains elusive, but apparently had something to do with Grandpa avoiding prosecution). The Goldsberry family made it to Ford County, Kansas where he found work on his brother Charlie's farm.

By 1939, the family was firmly settled in Dodge City when the beautiful sixteen-year-old Mary was invited to attend an event at the Pentecostal Holiness church in Sun City, Kansas. There she met a family named Chinn. Even in those days of larger families, a household of eleven kids would be impressive and memorable. Furthermore, every one of those kids was a vivid character of great panache and personality. One of the four Chinn boys was the good-looking, adventurous, face-to-the-wind Jack.

Five years later Jack Chinn and Mary Goldsberry were married. Two years after their wedding I was born (dead, as you may remember).

Very specific and pronounced factors—the Depression, World War II, Pratt County, the Chinn and Goldsberry legacies, our Pentecostalism, and the circumstances of my birth—all converged to form a terrible and wonderful matrix of growth for me.

In the 1950s, Pentecostalism didn't seem to do well in Kansas. It was like foreign grass; it just didn't take root and flourish in that cultural climate. Because there were so few Pentecostals and because it was viewed as a strange sect, I was often burrowed "in the closet." I had such an aching desire for acceptance. But, the shame of our Pentecostalism was ground into me like grease, mud, and muck into a farm house rug. Of course, our religion tried to redefine that shame as a badge of honor. *Just as the world rejected him, so it will reject us. Friendship with the world is hostility toward God. Beware when men speak well of you.*

But, these were heavy notions to lay on a kid who just wanted some friends. Much of my growing up was a cycle of daring to see, hear, touch, and taste, then pulling back in fear and shame. All my friends operated in wide freedoms regarding girls, sports, music, movies, cars, and the deeper zones of maleness like alcohol, smoking, and general farm country raunchiness.

So, for me, adolescence was a tumble through the faltering reaches and retreats, desires and disgraces. The cool sweet breeze of possibility so often turned into the foul stench of guilt for failing to "stand up for Jesus."

That cycle seemed to confirm that I was the object of a fierce struggle between heaven and earth. The Pentecostal Holiness

Church, my parents, and grandparents (in that order) were pulling me up to salvation. And, Steve Gilham, RC Watkins, and Margaret Moore's breasts (not in that order) were bent on hauling me down the road of sin. Of course, I had never actually seen her breasts. But I continually thought about them; I imagined them suddenly bursting free from their restraints and pushing out of her blouse, wet with passion and throbbing in my hands.

It was a vision infinitely more galvanizing than inviting Jesus into my heart.

But then just as the decade of the fifties came to a close, I sat in a typical and so-predictable Sunday morning service with RC Watkins and Ron Thomas. Suddenly, the very air began to take on an ominous tone, a dark atmospheric alteration, like a rapid change in barometric pressure. The silences became heavy. Too many heads were bowed. Too many Christian women were weeping. The atmosphere became so charged with "conviction," that the pastor, Delmar Becker, just stopped preaching. After a moment, he whispered "Let's just wait on the Lord."

The sweet tones of the inevitable "Softly and Tenderly" began floating out of the old piano. Waves of fear, then terror, then resignation, swept over me. I knew it was over (I mean, everyone knew that we were clearly the only "unsaved" people in the whole building). Brother Becker left the pulpit and was walking back toward us. I quickly looked away, straight into RC's eyes. They had a wide open, sky blue, *Oh shit* glaze. All three of us hit our knees. My face was flat against the butt-polished oak pew; my eyes were squeezed shut. The "saints" gathered around us as we "prayed through." Their hands kept jerking my head as though connected to high voltage wires. Folks were praying as they would if Russian missiles were screaming toward Pratt. I did not want this! The lusts of the flesh shook their heads in sad reflection of what-might-have-been as they slipped out the back door.

I wanted to go with them; I desperately wanted to be *out* of that place.

And, then, in a totally unexpected way, I *was* out of there. I could still hear and feel everything around me. But I was floating away to another place. Something in my chest broke loose and came gushing out my mouth in embarrassingly loud sobs. A very real *Presence* moved over me: confronting, accepting, convicting, forgiving, terrifying, comforting. And I was in full agreement with the Presence. My heart was bursting with a relief I didn't even know I needed. Joy filled my chest, my throat, and flowed out my eyes. I asked the Presence to save me and I meant it.

I was changed.

From that moment on, my personal story was part of a grand narrative, a river of salvation that cascaded down across the centuries and cultures. I knew who I was, I knew where I fit, I knew the rules. I was a Christian.

I grew into an understanding that the constructions and presumptions of Christianity were sacred space and everything else was profane and contaminated. God would just naturally come to the sacred spaces and he wanted no part of the spiritually polluted world. For me, the micro version of that meant that he would report promptly at 9:45 a.m. each Sunday morning and 7:00 p.m. each Sunday night and Wednesday night at that box we called First Pentecostal Holiness Church. It also meant we would never smoke, drink, go to movies, or dance.

That very logical and linear arrangement of my life remained intact for several years. In that time, I fell into easy conformity with the requirements and assumptions of my religious culture.

Chapter 3

CROSSING OVER

Four things happened between 1966 and 1973 which moved my heart across a boundary line that separated the claims and notions of an old world from the possibilities of a brand-new terrain.

First, I found the light and love of my life, Joanne, at our denomination's *Southwestern Bible School* in Oklahoma City. We were teenagers when we met and still teenagers when we married in 1965. Ten and a half months later, while living in San Marcos, Texas, Eddie was born. When I held this baby boy, looked into his eyes, and heard and felt the sounds warbling from him, I knew that much of what I had been told about God was, in fact, bullshit.

Fatherhood was a revelation to me; it delivered a serious shock to my religious paradigms. I knew that fatherhood on earth had to be, by some calculus, a reflection of God. And, I was just as sure that this little bundle of boy could never do anything in his life that would cause me to cast him away. I would have endless patience and mercy toward my child. Yet, I had picked up the assumptions of my religious culture that God was pretty angry and impatient with his kids; in fact, He was so pissed off that he was quite willing to toss them into the flames of hell.

For me, faith had always been a "High Noon" proposition. God, the Sheriff, instinctively knew that I was no good. And, naturally, He shared that perspective with everybody else in town. So, He and the good townspeople watched me continually, just waiting for me to violate one of the many ordinances of Heaven. Sadly, it was only a matter of time until I would face the Sheriff, standing in the dusty street. Like lightning, He would grab a fist full of gun and nail my immortal soul and leave it dying in the dirt. As He turned to the applause of good people everywhere, Satan would sweep my sorry ass off the street and cart me off to hell.

And, then one little baby invaded my heart, revealed new truths about God, and pulled down a pillar of my house.

Four years later, in August of 1970, we were living in Colorado Springs when a second old world pillar collapsed. I came to a sense of total failure as a husband, father, and man. At twenty-three, I was in debt, fearful, and unhappy. And even worse, Joanne was pregnant, a week past her delivery date and all baby movement had stopped. Total despair.

A moment is forever burned into my brain. I was running late for work because Joanne so desperately needed me. But, I couldn't afford to lose my job and insurance. I felt like I was being pulled apart; I finally just had to go. In tears, she followed me out to the car. As gingerly as I could, I pulled my arm from her desperate grip and drove away. I will always remember watching her grow smaller in my rear-view mirror, as she stood crying in the middle of the street. I loved her more than I had loved anything or anyone in my life. And, I had failed to bring her into a joy and fulfillment. She was hurting and it was because of me. But, it was larger than me; something somewhere was failing. A structure, a view, an approach to life was worthless and falling apart. This was serious.

I reached a new point of desperation. As I drove to work, I began to pray. Suddenly I just growled, "Lord, I may go to hell, but I will not live like this!" I was so angry and resolute and defiant that it scared me. But, something broke. I actually thought I heard something pop inside my head. A membrane burst and the Voice which had been so silent for so long whispered, "Welcome home, son." I remember struggling to stay on a road that was suddenly swimming.

A few days later, in a spooky echo from my own birth, a doctor came out and said the same words that my Dad had heard twenty-three years earlier, "Mr. Chinn, I'm sorry, but your baby is dead." And, for a second time in twenty-three years, I was the one who left the hospital alive. We had lost a baby, but I had broken through something and found life. An old and futile way was losing its grip on me. Very soon, Joanne would also be free of it.

A third pillar was seriously damaged one year later, in October of 1971, when Joanne and I took my parents on a vacation to Japan.

It was only twenty-seven years since the *Princeton* had been destroyed, killing many of Dad's friends and throwing him into his harrowing fight for survival. Naturally, he still carried very specific ideas about the Japanese (and, by inference, anyone who was threatening or even different). I noticed that he grew increasingly somber as we traversed the country. Of course, I could not realize the full meaning of his journey into the heartland of a still-vivid enemy.

After one day of sightseeing, we all emerged from the subway at Tokyo's Akasaka Station into a heavy rain. With no umbrellas, we faced a walk in the downpour to our hotel, which was two blocks away. Immediately, a well-dressed Japanese businessman came up behind my parents and held his umbrella over them. He got drenched as he so graciously and silently walked them all the way to our hotel. When we were all under the portico, he simply bowed and walked away. Dad shouted, "No, no, come back." The man turned and walked back to Dad.

In that moment, those two men—clearly about the same age

and undoubtedly veterans of the same war—stood face to face and shook hands. Neither said a word. But volumes passed between the eyes of the old warriors; each knew that he knew that he knew.

The son of one of those warriors saw it all. And what I saw that day, listening to the pouring rain, changed me deeply and permanently. My easy categorizations of "us vs. them" enforced by my religious cocoon and even by the values and attitudes my father had conveyed to me all took a mortal hit that day. Over time, they totally fell apart.

Two years later, in 1973, like a race car in a wet curve, I spun out of control and hit the wall; I came to the end of Ed (but certainly not for the last time). In addition to Eddie, we now had Paul and Amy. Joanne was amazing; I was not a good provider, but she didn't complain and she never demanded a thing. These should have been delightful years with our beautiful little family. But, I was sick of failure—at twenty-six years old, I kept going around the same damn mountain of debt and despair. I had a final break with religion. To hell with it. I was sick of religion's emphasis on the rules and the appearances. Like everyone else, I had learned how to maintain an external compliance with the rules. But, internally, I was a mess: confused, shallow, lustful, deceptive, irresponsible. Reality had finally blown a crater-sized hole through religion's heart.

But, this was more than just facing failure. I knew that real change would require a bold break with all that I knew. I was hyperventilating spiritually, desperate to climb out of my slimy comforts and ruts. My three-year-old prayer—"I will not live like this!"—continued to burn.

In November, we made a run for it. We left everything and moved to Pascagoula, Mississippi. I had earlier reached out to an old friend, Glen Roachelle, from *Southwestern Bible School* days. Glen was the best embodiment I'd yet seen of an Old Testament description of a Prince: one who is "a shelter from the wind and a refuge from the storm, like streams of water in the desert and the shadow of a great rock in a thirsty land (Isaiah 32:2 NIV)."

He was a leader in a Christian Community on the Gulf Coast of the US. In our starved and emaciated state, that community had become a hot cherry pie cooling in a farm house window. Its breeze created a delirium of desire.

It proved to be the best move we ever made. We found true community, enduring (to this day) friendships, emotional and marital healing, and a brand-new sense of success in life's essentials. Joy and health and a new prosperity began to surge through our home.

But, more than all that, for the first time in my life, I began to develop a completely different view of God. He was no longer the remote and angry Sheriff, but a living, touchable, discernable Personality. And, the Bible was alive! Reading the Bible was no longer a task; I couldn't wait to roll out of bed and grab that book.

Religion had convinced me that God's requirements come from heaven, but that the response had to come from me. That lie created a stinking pit of my best efforts and brightest ideas. But, in Pascagoula, I learned that I simply did have—was never designed to have—what it took to be a holy man. He was the only one who could live that kind of life and he would gladly do it through me. Good news: God was both, the requirement and the response. That was the turning point for me; I was his (not religion's and certainly not my own) creation.

So I quit. I somehow found the faith to give up. I basically told God that if he could live through me to go ahead.

Looking for Jesus

In the decades of my life since then, I have been on a playful, occasionally wrenching, journey through the dynamics of the God-man relationship. Spirit and flesh, lyrics and melody, poetry and prose. At times, the journey has been like shooting down a raging mountain stream. In other ways and times, I've felt more like a hunter quietly tracking The Grizzly. Sometimes, my journey has probably resembled that of a scientist searching for a cancer cure.

In this journey, I became and have remained fixated on Jesus. Who was, who is he? How did he handle that move from heaven to earth? Was he a normal kid during his time on earth? How did he balance the relationships between his heavenly Father and Joseph? Who taught him to fish? How did he relate to Mary? Did He ever do miracles as a kid? Was he drawn to the female form? What does "Body of Christ" mean? What does His Kingdom look like? What is the Church?

One cannot haul these questions around without meeting and mixing with those who call themselves "Christians." I bump into them all the time at conferences, in churches, at Starbucks. And, over the years of exploration of the God-man relationship, those questions even carried me into (and through) respectable and official positions in local churches. I wore the robes for a while, but never found one that fit.

In fact, I don't even think of myself as a Christian anymore. I'm in a quest for Jesus. To me, "Christian" seems to imply one who has found him and now embodies the character of Christ; the search is over. Turn out the lights; it's all established, institutionalized, crystallized and stuffed. Christianity is too often the mere taxidermy of Jesus. Furthermore, doesn't the label of "Christian" seem to unavoidably polarize us from everyone who is not? Somehow a broader and more inclusive identification of, I don't know, maybe . . . "earthling" is friendlier and more humble. It requires me to stand beside anyone on equal footing as a friend and fellow explorer.

I once heard Catholic theologian Ralph Martin say that the church should be a counterculture. After all, the church is supposed to be the embodiment of Jesus. And, he was the ultimate counter to dominant culture. The true Outsider. He came from Heaven to announce freedom for the captives and oppressed, healing for the broken and a brand-new life for the poor; he invaded the earthbound cultures of futility and enslavement with the countering claims and promises of his own alien government.

So, as I began to understand it, the church—his "body" in the earth—should/could live out those claims and promises, and would take up the causes and bear the burdens of the poor, the imprisoned, the oppressed and the broken. Yes! The church would display the upside-down difference he brought; it would invite all those marginalized and rejected people into his kingdom and then disciple them in the new freedoms and joys of Heaven on earth. The church would announce the generosity of God to the whole earth.

That was a vision worthy of investment!

And, since 1973, I've tried to do it (admittedly, not always well). However, I've also had to face the concurrent reality that the modern visible American institution which we call "church" often carries a different vision. Rather than filling a counterculture role, it has adapted to the prevailing patterns of consumerist American life.

Sadly, large parts of the church (primarily, some of the expressions of evangelicalism) have been good apprentices of the age. At last, they are fully certified agents of Western culture. America exalts progress as a virtue; so does the church. Our economy divides and disconnects; the church does it every bit as well. Dominant culture dismisses the poor and the powerless and exalts the rich and powerful. Too much of the church marches to the very same drumbeat (and is as hooked on "celebrity culture" as everyone else). Society worships technology. The church does too. Conformity is a premiere driving force in society; it moves even more relentlessly in the church.

Does any mature person really believe that the institution we call the church is in fact "His body, the fullness of him who fills all?" (Ephesians 1:23) If so, then why does the church—ostensibly the "Body of Christ"—act so independently of its head? Does Jesus suffer from spastic paralysis?

Or, is it possible that he has simply walked away? Could it be that he actually has no regard for the holy places we have built for him? Is he bored by our sacrifices and services? Maybe he really is a king and, as such, has a magnificent reign and work list.

Perhaps he sees the whole earth a holy place.

Chapter 4

REALITY AND SHADOWS

When we traded Colorado for Mississippi in 1973, we crossed the Rubicon which separated all that was known from a new frontier. Fittingly, our first stop on that road was Pratt, the territory of my theretofore sacred spaces. When we arrived, we drove straight to the Rock Island depot to see Dad. We knew he had been "called" and was about to board a train.

As I raced to embrace and stand beside my father, it became immediately clear that he was not happy about our move. For whatever reasons, he would not release and bless us into our new venture. He wouldn't even make eye contact with me as we stood together on the depot platform. The locomotive's looming enormity, its earth-trembling rumble, and petroleum stench overpowered my attempts to reach him. Finally, Dad just turned and walked away toward the caboose. It was like a paper cut to the heart. But, I let him go.

His very vivid rejection was both painful and liberating to me; the Rubicon River was now chest deep. I remember thinking *if I never see you again, it's an acceptable price to pay*. I was no longer Jack Chinn's little boy. Of course, I loved him dearly and his obvious rejection hurt like hell, but for the first time in my life I felt like a man. Instinctively I knew that if I would ever have any future with him, it would be on my own terms (I did and it was).

We drove into Pascagoula, Mississippi, our new hometown, on my twenty-seventh birthday. As we crossed the Pascagoula River Bridge on old US 90 (the city limit sign was in the middle of the bridge), I suddenly and unconsciously flipped the radio on. Immediately, John Denver's voice filled the truck cabin with these words:

He was born in the summer of his twenty-seventh year
Comin' home to a place he'd never been before
He left yesterday behind him
You might say he was born again
You might say he found a key for every door[12]

Certainly, I heard that song at that moment as a spine-chilling confirmation of our path (even in its curious concave reflection of us having just left the "Rocky Mountain High" of Colorado to be there). Everything in me took a deep sigh.

But, it was more than that. Coming as it did in the crossing into a new geography (literal and spiritual), that serendipitous moment was as clear as the PASCAGOULA CITY LIMITS sign we had just passed. We had left the land of religion and entered a zone where, over the years to come, we would find Heaven and earth joined in a pulse-pounding tango. God would no longer be confined to the convenient and safe expectations of religion. But, anytime and anyplace would bend to, dance with, and become a servant of his Presence. For example, he doesn't seem to need religious music as a conduit for his work. His truth will push right through Handel or Haggard, Mahalia Jackson or Michael Jackson.

Nor does he need those buildings we call "churches."

The Great Reality

A few months earlier, I had stood in a large room in Pueblo, Colorado with Glen Roachelle. We were speaking of spirit stuff.

---

[12] John Denver and Mike Taylor, *Rocky Mountain High* (Copyright 1972, Cherry Lane Music Co.)

To make a point, Glen thump-thumped one of the room's supporting pillars with his knuckles and said, "This wood post is only a shadow. The eternal realm is reality; every physical thing is a shadow cast by the eternal." *Epiphany*.

Similarly, A. W. Tozer once said, "All things are but shadows cast by the great Reality, God, and if we were to gain the whole world and miss God, we should have no more than a handful of shadows."

Over the years, I've stopped seeing God as the head of my (rather provincial) religion. At the risk of sounding generic or goofy, I've come to see God as "the great Reality." Like a rainstorm, he is magnificent, essential, entirely sufficient, wholly unmanageable, and terrifying. Throughout history, he has often been very personal in his dealings with people. We see him walking through a pool of animal and bird blood with Abraham; now his questions are being delivered with hurricane-force at Job, here he wrestles all night with Jacob (and leaves him crippled for life). This is one very intense God. Personal, face-to-face, intimacy with him is, at times, just too much. Small wonder that the human race must build storm shelters to absorb the occasionally-torrential fury of his Presence.

Is that the birthing room of religion?

The Religious Impulse

At its simplest, religion is a systematic belief in and approach to a big something or Someone (God, career, food, sex, etc.).

At its best, religion is a collective effort to obey God and transform his will into a "voltage" which can be used on earth. In other words, it seems to me that for religion to be valid it has to assume the perfection and power of God, take accountability to him seriously, and work to translate his will into noble and tangible results.

Because religion has, at times, fulfilled that nobility, millions of equipping or "second chance" institutions (like hospitals, colleges, orphanages, grantmaking foundations, homeless shelters, and food banks) have been built all over the earth. When religion focuses on God, it can be a point of "downloading" his beauty and wisdom into the desperation of human life. The Epistle of James confirms the role and value of that kind of religion: "Pure and undefiled religion before God and the Father is this: to visit orphans and widows in their trouble, and to keep oneself unspotted from the world." (James 1:27 NKJV)

I readily admit that such magnificence of religion continues today. Local churches respond in admirable ways to crises. I have nothing but respect for those churches and people who served community, nation, and planet so well in the aftermath of 9/11, tsunamis, hurricanes, and other national and natural calamities.

And, in the same way that foot paths become paved roads, religion has also built a wondrous "highway system" enabling many to travel more safely in their quest for God. The great creeds, hymns, monasteries, liturgies, and other inventions have permitted millions of pure and seeking souls to approach the Mountain of the Lord. At its best, religion can give voice to the reaching heart or handrails for weak and wobbly feet.

However, like any other God-man mixture, the "pure and undefiled religion" seems to become inevitably corrupted by the human touch. Something in my makeup always seems to screw me up, rendering me unable to simply receive and obey. I must control and improve.

Complication and confusion are the evidences that humans have been hanging around. I have learned to be wary and just STOP—kill the engine and just sit there a while—when things get confused or complicated . . . even when it comes from me.

A friend of mine once said, "You cannot have a photo of a tree; you always have a picture of what it was." In the same sense, I think religion usually captures an image of what once existed. It seems that the moment religion envisions God, he has slipped away into the new. Religion tends toward the old; often it is absolutely committed to the old. Some of the most powerful battles in history were fought by religion over the land and titles of the old way.

It seems to come down to this: religion can take a vertical or a horizontal view; it can be oriented to God or man. When religion looks up, it is helpful in translating the mysteries of Heaven for those on earth. However, when it only looks around on a horizontal plane, it stops being a response to Heaven and inexorably degenerates into a self-centered, self-serving arrangement. The orientation for religion should be toward the True North of obedience to God, not sensitivity to man. Of course, an orientation to God will usually command us to serve others. But, I think the sequence of that process is important.

God Has Come to Help!

I believe Jesus is the Son of the Father God and the "exact representation" of his Father's personality (Hebrews 1:3). In other words, when Jesus moved to earth, for the first time people got to see God walking around. That Awesome Personality, so long shrouded in dark clouds of mystery and myth, suddenly started showing up at parties, funerals, weddings, and work sites. As Eugene Peterson translates Revelation 21:3 in The Message, "God has moved into the neighborhood, making his home with men and women!"

Luke provided a revealing little vignette of what *God-with-us* must have looked like:

As he approached the town gate, a dead person was being carried out—the only son of his mother, and she was a widow. And a large crowd from the town was with her.

When the Lord saw her, his heart went out to her and he . . . touched the coffin, and those carrying it stood still. He said, "Young man, I say to you, get up!" The dead man sat up and began to talk, and Jesus gave him back to his mother.

They were all filled with awe and praised God. "A great prophet has appeared among us," they said. "God has come to help his people." (Luke 7:12-16)

Think of it: people watched as God felt—and then acted on compassion for an "earthling." They saw him raise her son from the dead and then give the boy back to her. He didn't try to recruit or exploit him for his "movement." Nor, oddly perhaps, did he even explore the mother or son's "spiritual condition." The people absorbed that scene, drew a clear and direct connection to Yahweh, and reached a conclusion that was both logical and astonishing: "God has come to help his people."

The Subversion of Religion

Millions believe that religion (Christian, Buddhist, Islamic, Jewish, Taoist, etc.) speaks for God. I think most people assume something like this: that the great religions are led by wise and holy and aged men (always men for some reason), lying prostrate before a burning Presence and listening to The Voice. *Mysterium Tremendum*. Or, they are buried far away in dark vaults studying (in flickering candle light) the cryptic and hallowed manuscripts of eternal wisdom. Then, with great judiciousness and fidelity, they translate and scatter that wisdom to and for the waiting mortals.

However, in reality, many of those imagined holy men are true nut cases, writing goofball theologies that deceive and behavioral codes that kill. So, in that sense, they are perjurers and traitors against the kind intentions of God. Of course, this treachery is most shockingly revealed in our times by pastors and priests who sexually or financially exploit their followers. And, here's a little secret: very few, if any, of these "shepherds" ever set out to violate those who followed them. I doubt that any of them built a conscious strategy to seduce or steal.

As a church consultant and former associate pastor, I've seen how religion so easily and so unknowingly becomes self-serving. Religion carries an attitude of entitlement. When you see yourself as part of an elite system, an alternate reality, it becomes easy to believe you are subject to different laws. Religion makes you bulletproof. Religion also has an internal dynamic which helps its leaders and other privileged ones to create a framework of life in which good things roll down toward themselves. They didn't mean to actually have sex with that little boy or their board chairman's wife; the framework of their life just caused them to come rolling down into their bed.

That's why one of the most radical statements about leadership ever written is a six-word line in Romans 15:3: ". . . even Christ did not please himself." And, so quite conversely, here is Jesus—*God-walking-around*—who could have indulged himself in and with anything on his own earth. However, the framework of his life was not constructed so as to cause the goodies to flow naturally down to himself.

Surely, this man was God!

The pure *bashfulness* of God's law was offensive to the Pharisees. They viewed law as a total prescription for individual and social life. And, God's approach seemed much too respectful of human space. In fact, one Bible scholar once called the law of God "modest." Did he actually mean to imply that it's not pervasive and total? Apparently, God does not see—never did see—law as an instrument of salvation. That could only come through the blood of a perfect sacrifice.

So, clearly, religion has often lied about the purpose and reaches of the law and, in fact, has tirelessly worked to hijack the whole idea of law as a means of controlling the environment for its own purposes.

Of course, this kind of subversion is not new. It has been going on for centuries. In fact, religion was a choking entanglement when Jesus appeared on the earth. Joseph Girzone summarizes the cultural environment very well in his book, *A Portrait of Jesus*:

> At the time of Jesus, people were burdened with layer upon layer of laws that regulated the smallest detail of daily life. Besides the oppressive laws of their Roman conquerors, there was a body of Jewish law, civil and religious. And among the religious laws there were not just ten commandments. There were 613 commandments and 365 prohibitions, and many hundreds lesser injunctions that people had to follow. When they could not measure up to these ideals, the religious leaders excommunicated them and cut them off from the society . . . [13]

No wonder people are cynical about religion. Too much of religion carries a history of lying about God, manipulating and exploiting and oppressing people. And, we all know that too many religious professionals engage in the worst kinds of self-enrichment. Plus, it's a helluva lot to remember.

A religious friend once said to me, "you seem to be a reader, but I've never heard you mention any book that I would consider Christian. Do you read Christian books?"

---

[13] Joseph F. Girzone, *A Portrait of Jesus* (New York: Doubleday, 1998) p. 13

I thought about it for a moment, but had to admit: "Rarely."

"Then, how do you know the best ways to serve God?"

It was a fair question and one I had frankly never considered. I had to think and stumble through the answer, "Well, I guess in the same way that I've never read a book on how to farm. I learned that from my Grandfather."

The Choice

For me, at last, spiritual life all came down to the same issue: Did I hunger for bread or books by those who had reportedly eaten or baked it? Did I want a living and warm relationship or academic exercises?

Did I need footprints I could track, photograph, and research? Or, was I searching for life, a Life that often made its way through the sea?

Here is a true conundrum: Jesus is the reliable and resplendent view of the Father God, while religion has proven to be a liar about him. Religion makes me jump through hoops and work my tail off to be accepted and approved. Jesus paid the price of my acceptance, has fully and unconditionally approved me, and will live through me.

Why is this a difficult choice?

And, yet it is.

People regularly choose religion's "handful of shadows" over the Great Reality. Is that because he is so terrifying? Are we so addicted to control that we cannot relate to the Unmanageable One? Or, have we become so sensual in our perceptions that we no longer even detect the deeper and quieter nuances of his Presence?

Why do we insist on watering our garden during a thunderstorm?

An honest look at those questions leads inevitably to the church. I think that is because we have a cultural consensus that the visible church is the voice which speaks for God. It is his "agent"; you have to go through the church if you want to have a meeting with God. Or, the church is seen as God's PR guy. You want a quote about him? Stick a mike and camera in the face of a local pastor or religion professor. We think they know. The consensus would never go to a commercial fisherman, an IRS agent, or someone living in marginal morality for an "expert" view of God. Yet, those are the very people who comprised Jesus' circle of friends.

That cultural consensus has led to illusions of enormous impact. In considering those illusions, I decided to go back to his first appearance on the earth.

Chapter 5

THE LIGHT OF THE WORLD

Jesus was born into a time and place that was complicated, harsh, burdensome, and unforgiving. The people of Nazareth lived under the dual oppressions of Roman conquerors and the extensive and growing web of Jewish religious and civil law. Even in that time, religion was well into its path of perjury and treason against Heaven. It wore the robes of virtue and supremacy and was quite adept at using them to confirm the rules of the realm.

When we attempt to go back and view the appearance of Jesus on the earth, we so often have to look through a lens that is badly smudged with far too many fingerprints. It is very complicated and confusing.

But, in truth, His appearance is as simple and clear as a big yard light shining out into the darkness of the farm. That could be why he is called the "Light of the world."

From the moment that Light dawned out of the body of the virgin, it continued to burn brighter and brighter. As it slowly began to reveal previously unseen colors, textures, movements and motives, a whole new reality started to throb and emerge.

The Light began to glow behind the far mountains and then the sky slowly turned from black to purple to blue. At last, the Light broke the horizon and burned into the gutter of death that darkness had incubated in the earth. The Light continued to roll across the landscape. Finally, one day in Nazareth, the Light reached the Synagogue. It was there, in Jesus' earthly hometown, that the Light of the World turned his gaze on that intimidating power center of religion. When The Robes handed him the book that day, he read from one they esteemed, Isaiah. They probably didn't even see it coming:

> "The Spirit of the Lord is upon me; he has appointed me to preach Good News to the poor; he has sent me to heal the broken-hearted and to announce that captives shall be released and the blind shall see, that the downtrodden shall be freed from their oppressors, and that God is ready to give blessings to all who come to him."
>
> He closed the book and handed it back to the attendant and sat down, while everyone in the synagogue gazed at him intently. Then he added, "These Scriptures came true today!" (Luke 4:18-21, The Living Bible)

In those very few words, everything was suddenly turned upside-down. Jesus had announced new terms of life. The old rules and the old rulers were out. The intimidations of religion were dead, shot through the heart. It's been doing a slow-motion fall into the dirt ever since that day.

The light rays of that word must have flashed right into the dungeons and leper colonies and prisons and squalid huts. The sharp inhalation of surprise. Souls sitting chained in darkness stirred with new life. *Maybe. Could it be? Is that the voice of a brand new day?*

But, there in the council of the strong, his words stirred something else. Plunged into sudden chaos, they didn't know much, but they certainly knew that something big had just slammed into the south side of their house. Amidst the dust and debris, their first words were desperate and dazed attempts to regain control.

"Oh," the old order nodded, "He is a . . . a good speaker. Yes. He has a grasp of the language." Then, the frowns and furrowed brows. "But . . . listen, isn't he Joseph's boy? I know he's the young man who works there in that shop; he would have to be Joseph and Mary's son." And, another lowered his voice, looked over his shoulder, stroked his beard, and growled in a whisper, "Well, remember, he's not Joseph's. Reeling and reaching for the handrails, the snarls began slowing forming "*bas-tard*."

The light had caught the old guard of religion as a badger, wild-watery-eyed and fangs bared, fighting in the corner for his rabid life. The stench of his fear was palpable.

But, then the words started up again.

> "...remember how Elijah the prophet used a miracle to help the widow of Zarephath-a foreigner from the land of Sidon. There were many Jewish widows needing help in those days of famine, for there had been no rain for three and a half years, and hunger stalked the land; yet Elijah was not sent to them.
>
> Or think of the prophet Elisha, who healed Naaman, a Syrian, rather than the many Jewish lepers needing help." (Luke 4:25-27, The Living Bible)

With those words, Jesus told them that their grip, religion's grip, had cracked and would crumble. Their historic culture-lock was now worthless. Furthermore, all the patterns of expectation (such as their confidence that God would help Jewish widows before helping foreigners) had changed. In the future, nothing would go the way of their assumptions (like God favored the Jews over Syrians). Their ethical and moral systems were junk. Throw them away; they will never work again. God's generosity is larger than anyone ever imagined and he will pour it out anytime and anywhere he chooses. Get used to it: religion has no role in that distribution.

The implications of that announcement were (and are) profound and unfathomable. The reach of his words would change every calculation—spiritual, moral, ethical, political, and economic.

Religion's *terra firma* jumped; dust billowed out around the edges of its world view. Light brought a new order of life and terms of surrender for the old. Later, some would remember that his mother had caught a glimpse of that new order; her spirit opened up one day and she groaned—groaned it out as though it had already happened: "He has torn princes from their thrones and exalted the lowly. He has satisfied the hungry hearts and sent the rich away with empty hands." (Luke 1:52-53, The Living Bible)

But back to the story; at that point, the badger had no choice. It went for the throat.

> "…all in the synagogue were filled with rage as they heard these things; and they rose up and cast Him out of the city, and led Him to the brow of the hill on which their city had been built, in order to throw Him down the cliff." (Luke 4: 28 - 29 NASB)

Jesus may have rolled along with the mob in order to study the face of religion a little longer. I wonder if he stared into those gnarled, seething and spitting faces, and just shook his head in amused irony. But, then, perhaps bored, when they got to the cliff, he slipped away. Disappeared. He had other things to do. Luke finishes the story with the understated conclusion: "He went on His way." Not the old way, not their way. His way.

Strangest thing; sometimes Jesus just disappears. At the historical moment, when all eyes are on Him and greater things are within reach, He vanishes. Mark told another story of one of his disappearances:

> Very early in the morning, while it was still dark, Jesus got up, left the house and went off to a solitary place, where he prayed. Simon and his companions went to look for him, and when they

found him, they exclaimed: "Everyone is looking for you! ' Jesus replied, "Let us go somewhere else . . ." (Mark 1:35-38 NIV)

Among other things, the term "Light of the world" means that he appears wherever and whenever and for as long as he chooses. The rays of that Light fall across kingdoms and cultures and civilizations according to his own will and wisdom. Of course, when light remains in one place for a while, the particular environment begins to assume that it owns or contains the light. It doesn't.

The contemporary church is one of the best examples of that truth.

The word "church" is almost a homograph (one word—like "lead"—which carries two different meanings). We use that one word "church" to define, both, a timeless and invisible mystery and a cultural and very visible institution. The institutional church works feverishly to borrow legitimacy from the timeless church. True to the way of all flesh, that borrowed authenticity has produced illusions. One of the illusions nourished by the institutional church is that it owns the light. In fact, one of the grand intellectual heists of all time is the idea that *the visible church*—the buildings, the programs, the advertising, the belief systems—is indistinguishable from the light. As it always has, this is simply the religious impulse attempting to impose a self-serving lock on its environment.

In fact, the visible or institutional church does not own him any more than the earth owns the sun. The light of the sun falls across the entire earth. And, it keeps moving over the face of the earth. Light, by the very nature of God and his creation, will always appear and then disappear. It is never captured or controlled. It originates somewhere else and invades our world. We never hold on to it.

I don't know if anyone else has noticed, but I think the Light has disappeared. It has moved on . . . again.

The river of my life and work has carried me through many churches over the years.[14]   In those years, I've filled many church roles: disciple, associate pastor, administrator, member, visitor, and a consultant and guide. I've experienced a wide diversity of American churches: large and small, traditional and radical, dying and inceptive, urban and suburban, wealthy and poor, Caucasian and non, liberal and orthodox, modern and post. In church, I've been mesmerized, heartbroken, mad as hell, carried away to Heaven, and clinically bored.

I first began to suspect that God had left the building a few years ago. Several things began to get my attention. For example, I noticed that . . .

Pastors and parishioners kept doing and saying the same things. Local churches—from pulpit to pew—were bubbling cauldrons of clichés. I could foresee every phrase. To some degree this is always true of institutions.   But this was different; I saw that churches were profoundly locked on autopilot and caught in a cultural rut (and one distinctive of his Presence is that the atmosphere remains fresh, creative, and electric).

God is so creative. Consider that he only did the "Red Sea" thing once. Did it and apparently forgot it. Never needed it again in all of history (if I were God, I'd have done it quite a bit). So, how is it that those ostensibly "born again" into his kingdom trudge along in such mind-numbing conformity and outright plagiarism? For example, one day a minister suddenly asked those standing before him to turn to others and form circles of prayer. I'm sure

---

[14] As an American, my observations are limited to the church in America. However, because American culture is so dominant in the earth, the same characteristics exist in churches of other nations.

it was inspired and lovely. But, why did that take on a life of its own and become "liturgized?" Now, it happens thousands of times all across the country every Sunday morning.

I also saw that other stuff was becoming central: political and social issues, structure, worship styles, doctrine, children, seniors, and "how-to-do-church models," whatever. It seemed that almost anything was replacing him in the center of his own church. Hardly anyone seemed to be honestly listening, watching, or waiting for him. The local church had developed a momentum which seemed wholly independent of him.

Jesus is reality. Yet, it seemed to me, that in a church that calls itself by his name, a great gorge began to split the ground between words and action. Church life became all about the moment and the event. Words were used as cue balls—to cause certain effects. Truth was removed from language. Words lost their content, context and continuum. It became increasingly clear to me that reality, real life, was slipping away.

In my travels, I also began to notice that people were too busy, distracted, and preoccupied with *activity*. They appeared to be enslaved to something—finances, relationships, perhaps even the church itself. People were working very hard and feverishly doing and saying things with no apparent purpose except perhaps to control the atmosphere and keep intimacy away. The noted philosopher Jacques Ellul warned that the thrust of modern life "is entirely directed toward action . . . our world is so obsessed by activity that it is in danger of losing its life." [15]

A crucial evidence of this loss of real life is in the way the church has forgotten any semblance of the Sabbath. For too many, church life on Sunday is closer to a slaughterhouse than it is to a Sabbath. Family life is shredded. Rest, personal reflec-

---

[15] Jacques Ellul, *The Presence of the Kingdom* (Colorado Springs: Helmers & Howard Publishers, 1989) p. 74

tion, and gratitude are frequently slain on an altar of programs and meetings.

But, I suppose the most all-encompassing sign of his disappearance was in the reduction of him to property. Just as religion once tried to capture and catalog him as the hometown boy, "the carpenter's son," he has become "our" Jesus. We understand him, define him, control him, improve him, and market him. He hasn't surprised or challenged us in years. He hasn't wrecked the furniture in *our* temple or made us wet *our* pants in a very long time. He's our buddy; he goes along with whatever we want. He believes what we believe. He votes for our guy. He feels our pain. He indulges our consumer compulsions. He completely understands the uniqueness of our sin.

But, the real Jesus is the plumbline, the Personification of truth, and he hangs down throughout all history and civilizations. He is a supreme monarch, The King. He initiates; he doesn't react. He is the Progenitor, the Fountainhead of all things. Jesus always cuts across my thoughts, my plans, my needs, my life.

When Jesus chose one disciple, the man quickly agreed but asked permission to go to his father's funeral before proceeding. Jesus did not understand this reasonable request. He said, "Let the dead bury their own." Another guy was quick to sign up, but said he'd be right back after telling his family good-bye. Jesus did not understand; he meant right now.

That Jesus has disappeared from the village, the landscape, and the parallel universe of the contemporary, western, Christian experience. In his place, we are left with our own created "folk religion," that synthesis of American individualism, destructive consumerism, and self-aggrandizing patriotism that we call "faith."

Chapter 6

WHO IS HE?

One of the biggest problems in looking at Jesus is that we can't. We simply do not have reliable imagery of his face, or fresh vignettes of his personality, or contemporary and certifiable presentations of his attitudes. Everything we know about him is filtered through a couple millenniums of stained glass and religious traditions. We want to know, but we do not know, how he would live in our times.

Because of that cultural and intellectual vacuum, he is often a large blank projection screen; we throw up anything we want, call it Son of God, and use it to enforce our own self-serving motives. Whattayaknow, he is just like me.

Jesus knew that would happen. That may be why he asked his disciples, "Who do you say that I am?" That question still faces us. Because he is and will always be Spirit, we will never get firm coordinates on him. He will always be somewhat like "Bigfoot." We'll hear certain sounds, catch glimpses of what may or may not be Jesus (like the Shroud of Turin), and read reports by those who swear they had a face-to-face meeting ("Yeah, He smelled kinda like cinnamon, apples, and the land after a rain.").

The problem in "locating" him is that we're too sensual. We need smell, touch, sight, sound, and taste. Desperately we want something conclusive and incontestable. That's part of the problem. We want that "foreverness" of irrefutable, "take-*that*-you-idiot" evidence so that we can subdue "them" and vindicate ourselves.

If we can just fully identify him and his values, then unbelieving old Uncle Bob or Hillary Clinton and all other "pagans" will be reduced to a slobbering mass, jerking on the floor like frying bacon, screaming that they've been wrong, and begging us to help them find the way.

But, he never gives us that sensual satisfaction. He is Spirit. His walk way is through the ocean; his footsteps splash across the surface or swirl a cloud of bottom sand and silt that leaves no print and no sound. We think he was here; we're not sure. We can't find any trace.

Those of us who attempt to follow Christ tend to live in a grid of definitions, boundaries, requirements, and codes called "Christianity." We also live in an assumption that Jesus was a Christian. He wasn't. One of the most absurd titles assigned to Jesus, usually found in encyclopedias or religious histories, is "Founder of Christianity."

Christianity is man's organized attempts to domesticate and shrink Jesus. He has no part of that. He is no more the founder of Christianity than rain is of umbrellas. He is the ultimate Outsider.

Many Christians have a parental impulse toward him. We want people to like, trust, and follow him—after all, he's "our" Jesus. When they challenge or insult or ignore him, we take it very personally. That parental impetus reveals that we do not know him. We only know our private, narcissistic, projection of him.

The English preacher Charles Spurgeon (1834 - 1892) remains one of the few writers who have captured a reasonable profile of Jesus. Spurgeon's own visage—cigar smoking, lion-faced, beard-like-a-rockslide, mountain man—may provide clues to why he seems to understand the masculine grandeur of Jesus. Living as we do in an age which has so miniaturized the Christ, we ought to read more of Spurgeon. Yes, his style is dated. But what a vivid portrait this real man painted of the real Jesus, the One Who rides history like a stallion:

> Our Redeemer's glorious cry of "It is finished" was the death-knell of all the adversaries of His people . . .

> Behold the hero of Golgotha using His cross as an anvil, and His woes as a hammer, dashing to shivers bundle after bundle of our sins, those poisoned "arrows of the bow"; trampling on every indictment, and destroying every accusation.

> What glorious blows the mighty Breaker gives with a hammer far more ponderous than the fabled weapon of Thor! How the diabolical darts fly to fragments, and the infernal bucklers are broken like potters' vessels! Behold, He draws from its sheath of hellish workmanship the dread sword of Satanic power! He snaps it across His knee, as a man breaks the dry wood of a branch, and casts it into the fire. Beloved, no sin of a believer can now be an arrow mortally to wound him, no condemnation can now be a sword to kill him, for the punishment of our sin was borne by Christ, an atonement was made for all our iniquities by our blessed Substitute and Surety.

> . . . Jesus has emptied the quivers of hell, has quenched every fiery dart, and broken off the head of every arrow of wrath; the ground is strewn with the splinters and relics of the weapons of hell's warfare, which are only visible to us to remind us of our former danger, and of our great deliverance. Sin hath no more dominion over us. Jesus has made an end of it, and put it away for ever . . .[16]

If we are honest about it *that* Jesus scares the hell out of us. He is so large and his strength is so harrowing that our own self-interests drive us to make him safer, smaller, and more manageable. So, we work on him until he gradually morphs into our

---

[16] Charles Spurgeon, *Morning and Evening*, June 11 (http://www.ccel.org/s/spurgeon/morn_eve/morn_eve.html)

own image, an image that is comfortable to us—he is Jesus the androgynous, Jesus as Oprah, Jesus the environmentalist, Jesus the Republican. At last, he has become the ultimate confirmation of our own values and attitudes.

Trouble, Trouble Right Here in River City

Very often when God steps onto the earth, disaster erupts. New canyons split the landscape, water rises, flames lick at our dreams, trains and careers end in wreckage, cancer and heart attacks start escorting people to the other side.

Faith is the wholehearted embrace of that; it signs us on for the whole journey. In so doing, it makes us long-term students of his almighty largeness. Faith knows there is more going on here than meets the senses. Because of that, real faith doesn't assume or dictate, but rather changes the one in whom it dwells. Faith stands in the burned out shell of the family home or in the bankruptcy court or in the mortuary and keeps gazing into the face of God. Faith absorbs the blast of instruction from eternal council without making rash or permanent judgments. As it does so, faith slides the faithful man or woman from a finite earthbound view over to a surpassing heavenly one.

But, religion is too often a mere defense mechanism. It constructs a bunker around Me and Those Like Me and demands that life make sense from our perspective; it imposes a self-serving rationality on the circumstances. Often, however, there is none. That's why Paul admitted that sometimes we are just "perplexed." (II Corinthians 4:8). Sometimes that is all you can be or say. It is the creature's only honest summary of life.

There are few natural displays as awesome and wonderful as a lightning storm. The sheer electrical power of a lightning bolt surpasses our comprehension. Naturally, we all prefer that electricity be domesticated and subservient to our purposes. And civilization (thanks to Thomas Edison) has done a good job at doing that. But lightning still explodes into mountains, sets forests aflame, and kills people and livestock.

Jesus is lightning; Christianity is a 110-volt receptacle. That domestication isn't bad. In fact, it's inevitable. But, like other features of civilization, it causes us to forget the source and sweep of truth. By living in the "harnessed" realm of faith, we tend to lose sight of the enormous and majestically uncontainable reality that is Jesus. Worse, like the taming of electricity, Christianity conveys the illusion that we own the Christ.

The Stumbling Block

I don't think that Jesus came to earth in response to human need or initiative. Humanity didn't want, understand, or ask for him. And man will never be comfortable with the real Jesus (any more than we will ever be comfortable in a lightning storm). By his very nature, Jesus cuts across history, civilizations, and all human plans and desires. He is an offense, a scandal, a stumbling block.

For example, when some read about him making wine, they concoct strange rationalizations to make him less offensive . . . well, it wasn't real wine, it wasn't actually fermented like it is today, etc. And, let's face it; we would have liked him better if he'd told the woman at the well to move out on the guy she was living with. We want him to heal people's bodies, give them new jobs, fix their marriages, etc. Sometimes he does. Sometimes he doesn't.

He is a King. In the large sense, what we think or feel really doesn't matter; the only issue is what he thinks (and how we align and harmonize with that). And that may be the biggest distinction between the real Jesus and the one manufactured by Christianity.

The artificial Jesus wants to be liked and understood. Therefore, all that he does makes sense to us, comforts us, and confirms us. He never disturbs us.

Yet, Jesus is a profound disturbance.

When he appeared on earth, babies were murdered. When he came through one village, a herd of swine hurled themselves into the sea. His life on earth would bring swords and the disintegration of families; furthermore, he disparaged family peace and unity for the higher call of discipleship. He drank alcohol, socialized with prostitutes and sinners, and slept in the woods. He quickly gained and kept a bad reputation with the religious order; He was known as a "glutton, a drunkard, and a friend of sinners."

I sometimes cringe when I read things he said or did. There is something about him that violates respectability. He seems a little too direct with followers (I wish he had allowed the new guy to go bury his own father). He actually told people to eat his flesh and drink his blood (I think I could have helped him say that a little better). Jesus once cursed a fig tree because it didn't have any figs even though it was not the season for produce. At times, he seemed disdainful (even rude) to His mother, family, and hometown folks. And, he even called one of his closest friends "Satan."

When he heard that his friend and cousin John was in prison, Jesus apparently turned and departed in the opposite direction. In fact, John was beheaded without ever seeing him. Did Jesus even recognize the inconsistency of promoting compassion toward prisoners (Matthew 25:36-40) while failing to do so himself? Did he even care about what that would do to his cousin and other relatives? Obviously, the forsaken John went through some dark nights of the soul over that; he sent a delegation to ask if Jesus really was

The One. It is significant that Jesus concluded his conversation with John's emissaries by saying, "Go tell John . . . blessed is he who keeps from stumbling over Me." (Matthew 11:6).

The message was clear. Jesus came from somewhere else. His ways were often unintelligible and offensive to earthlings. He knew he was a stumbling block to many. And He wouldn't make it easy for them. He only had three years to accomplish his mission; things had to be done. Those who possessed the faith to keep pressing in without stumbling would find themselves blessed; they would pass beyond themselves. They would find the lift essential to rising above the suffocating confines of their own preferences.

An Unlikely Leader

I personally think that one of the major stumbling block factors is that Jesus was simply not the embodiment of our idea of a Savior. As you read the Gospels, you do not see a man trying to build a movement or even win adherents. Rather, when some people revealed interest in following him, He threw up roadblocks to discourage them. In fact, when it appeared that some kind of grass-roots movement was starting, that people were taking notice of new leadership, Jesus said, "Let's go somewhere else . . . "

As he often does, he disappeared.

And, that is so offensive to us because we all want to be wanted. We want leaders to ask for our support. We want them to court us. Our raging ego demands that we be considered as attractive candidates for inclusion in a movement. The key to Jesus' leadership is found in John 5:30 where he said, "I can do nothing on My own initiative . . . I do not seek My own will, but the will of Him who sent Me."

I think that everything that Jesus did or said was initiated by his Father in Heaven. Jesus was only accountable to One. Human response was never a measurement of his mission. In fact, he didn't even trust the earthlings (he was under no illusions about the content of their heart); he didn't have to trust them. Their responses or trustworthiness had nothing to do with his purpose on earth. He was the King of the universe on an official visit to the planet earth. Jesus came at the direction and pleasure of his father. In doing so, he stepped into the rebellious realm and simply obeyed. That impossible-to-comprehend obedience altered the historical course of disobedience, defeated sin and death, and announced terms of life and terms of surrender.

Maybe that's why he never tried to lead anyone to himself. He never gave "an altar call" or asked anyone to "receive me into your heart." He was operating on a universal and historic platform, dealing with ancient and domineering principalities. When Jesus healed people of diseases, he wasn't doing it because of their need or to get them to follow. I think he was simply demonstrating— perhaps even studying—the practical collapse of that wheezing, arthritic power of death in the earth.

A friend of mine was leaving a restaurant. As he approached one table, a man sitting at that table began having some kind of fit; his face contorted and he began growling and snarling. It was a truly frightening spectacle. As my friend walked by, he simply laid his hand on the man's shoulder and said, "Hush!" The man was instantly transformed into a picture of peace. My friend walked on out the door and left. He didn't need to speak further. He didn't need to "close the sale." What he did was enough—he acted upon the victory resident in the earth because Jesus once walked this same dusty realm.

No area represents the deep chasm between the Christ and Christianity more than this one. Jesus operates from a position of victory. He doesn't need to see a human validation of that victory. Those of us who call ourselves Christians usually operate from defeat and insecurity. We do need some kind of validating response from those like us.

Jesus was always looking to Heaven; we tend to look no higher than those standing around us. That critical difference has led to a full embrace of marketing philosophy in the church. We must reach *them*. We assume that our success is measured by how many of *them* become like us. That false assessment has been extracted into the details of how many "Christian" CDs and books are sold, how many NFL players and coaches are Christians, the ticket receipts for Christian concerts or movies, and how many "decisions for Christ" are made in a given church, city, or nation within a year.

He is Spirit

When Joseph went through his understandable struggle about his fiancé's pregnancy, an angel told him to go ahead and "take Mary home as your wife, because what is conceived in her is from the Holy Spirit." (Matthew 1:20 NIV). That statement is one of the highest peaks along the continental divide of history.

Very Man was also Very God. Perhaps the largest stumbling block factor is that Jesus is Spirit. If you don't believe that, consider this passage of scripture (John 6:54-68 NAS) where Jesus said,

> "He who eats My flesh and drinks My blood has eternal life . . . For My flesh is true food, and My blood is true drink. He who eats My flesh and drinks My blood abides in Me, and I in him . . ."

These things He said in the synagogue, as He taught in Capernaum. Many therefore of His disciples, when they heard this said, "This is a difficult statement; who can listen to it?"

> But Jesus, conscious that His disciples grumbled at this, said to them, "Does this cause you to stumble? . . . It is the Spirit who gives life; the flesh profits nothing; the words that I have spoken to you are spirit and are life . . . For this reason I have said to you, that no one can come to Me, unless it has been granted him from the Father."
>
> As a result of this many of His disciples withdrew, and were not walking with Him anymore. Jesus said therefore to the twelve, "You do not want to go away also, do you?"
>
> Simon Peter answered Him, "Lord, to whom shall we go? You have words of eternal life.

To the earth-ear, Jesus' statements about eating his flesh and drinking his blood are deeply and outrageously offensive. The imagery conjured by the words is grotesque and disgusting. Jesus knew that this statement was stumbling block stuff. And, sure enough, it peeled some followers away. At that point, Jesus turned to "the twelve" and asked if they were leaving too. Peter's ice-cold realism essentially said,

"Well tell me Jesus, just where the hell would we go? Your words have already taken root and taken over our heart. We are no longer our own. We're ruined for anything else; we've burned all our bridges and boats. Looks like we'll be staying with you. You're the only source of life we have or could imagine."

One of the most evocative lines in scripture is Luke 24:32. The scene is after the crucifixion; two of Jesus' disciples were walking down a road when he joined them. But, because of the changes in his appearance, they didn't recognize him. As they walked, he began to speak Spirit words. Finally, they sat somewhere. And, there he took bread, broke it, and served it to them. They recognized him (what an utterly sublime moment that must have been as his earlier word—"He who eats my flesh and drinks my blood abides in me, and I in him—echoed through their hearts). Upon recognition, he instantly disappeared. And, they turned to each other, probably nodding their heads in awe, and said, "Were not our hearts burning within us while he was speaking to us on the road, while he was explaining the Scriptures to us?"

The clinical and sterile portraits of Jesus tend to focus on his "teaching" as if he merely developed a new philosophy. Or, he is viewed as a revolutionary, one who started a grassroots movement that convulsed the socioeconomic order. These sketches miss him by a mile. He was/is Spirit. His voice sets the heart on fire. His words are like seeds; when they fall into human soil, they sprout! They crowd "me" out; they take over. When His unmistakable voice crashes into time and space, people weep or fall down or think they're having strokes. Something happens! A Spirit-voice reverberates throughout the environment and the physical order—even the human body—begins to shimmer and shake and move around. Nothing will ever be the same again.

Of course he is a stumbling block. We live in the realm of earth and are only really comfortable with the small personalities and issues which emerge from the earth. Anything or Anyone from the other side intimidates and frightens us. This is especially true because of the damage to our own way that occurs whenever God steps into our realm. We're like the citizens of Matthew 8: after Jesus stepped into their realm and so destabilized the atmosphere that their swine plunged into the sea, they begged him to get out of town. Perhaps more to the point, we're like Peter, a disciple, a deeply flawed man who tried his best to follow. When Jesus stepped into his boat and caused the natural order to fill Peter's nets to fill up with fish, Peter told him to get out of his boat. Jesus is simply too large, too troublesome, too unmanageable, too disturbing, too Heaven-oriented, and too spiritual for our earthiness to ever fully embrace him.

He is history's great stumbling block.

Chapter 7

THE LORD OF THE WHOLE EARTH

In being born as a baby and growing up as a human, God had to stoop down to enter the cramped cave called earth. That is surely the most astonishing story ever told . . . God became a human. Yet right there is where the traditional telling of the story goes a little haywire. We work so hard to shrink him down that we end up only seeing him from a human perspective. By that, we lose sight of the purpose and nature of his incarnation.

He is not primarily "baby Jesus, meek and mild." He is the Monarch of all created order; he came to earth on an official State Visit. Jesus stooped down to enter because he had to; he was too tall for our flesh-door. As any king might stoop down to enter a vassal's dwelling, so this king had to duck in order to come into our home. We call that "ducking" the Incarnation. But, He never stopped being a Monarch. Not for one second.

Simeon and Anna understood that. The beautiful story told in Luke 2 reveals an historic moment. The temple was full of babies that day as it had been every day for the past few decades of these elderly people's lives. Babies were always being presented to God in the temple. But, when Simeon and Anna saw this baby, they didn't tickle his chin and baby talk to him. After seeing babies for decades, on this day, these holy and resolute people pulled back the little blanket and saw the king of all creation, ducking down to enter the earth (I wonder if he winked at them).

And, consider the bewildering scene twelve years later. In his first recorded disappearance, Jesus vanishes from Mary and Joseph's sight. They search everywhere, but cannot find the boy. He's gone for three days! When they finally find him, he's not playing ball and he's not being a tourist; he's in the temple talking with the teachers. This is how Eugene Peterson translates the scene:

> The teachers were all quite taken with him, impressed with the sharpness of his answers. But his parents were not impressed; they were upset and hurt. His mother said, "Young man, why have you done this to us? Your father and I have been half out of our minds looking for you."
>
> He said, "Why were you looking for me? Didn't you know that I had to be here, dealing with the things of my Father?" (Luke 2:47-49, "The Message")

This is not a docile "Christian" boy. Nor is this a defiant child of the age talking back to his parents. Rather, this is the King of all creation, looking at his work list for the next twenty years of his royal visit to this planet. In the midst of that, he now has to deal with these increasingly tiresome earthlings who are approaching the end of their appointed service. For just a moment, the curtain of flesh parted and anyone watching would have seen the Sovereign Monarch correcting two of his subjects on their use of the word "father."

What does Lord mean?

Mary and Joseph made the same mistaken assumption about him that people have been making for two thousand years. *He is supposed to be with us.* We all have some perceived, even ostensibly reasonable, "rights" to him (like Mary and Joseph's supposed "parental rights"). And, according to our unspoken assumptions, he is obligated to conform to those rights. Like Mary and Joseph, we all have a very tough time with his disappearances. When He vanishes, it upsets the order of our expectations, violates our illusion of control, and reminds us of his lordship.

The word translated as "Lord" in Luke 2:29 (and other New Testament passages) means "One who has absolute ownership and uncontrolled power." This is not complicated: he answers to no one; his power and authority are not subject to anyone's control. That reality includes his prerogative to appear or disappear as he chooses.

As Christians, we may assume that he is supposed to be with us in our culturally-derived meeting places (those buildings we call "churches") and times (Sunday morning at 10:00 a.m.). But, he is the Lord. He may or may not be there. And, we can recite whatever incantations we want ("well, folks, the word promises that where two or three are gathered together, he will be there . . ."), but he's the Sovereign Lord. He has his own purposes and initiatives. And they are global in scope; he is the Lord of all the earth.

Yes, I do believe Jesus will honor his promises to be with us. But, too often, we allow human need to climb into the driver's seat and assume some creature-power over the Creator. We should never forget who he is and the unfathomable scope of his purpose and work list.

More than a husband

The great Bible teacher Charles Simpson once said, "The church is Jesus' bride, but she's not his whole life." As a husband, I get it. I love Joanne very much, but I have realms of responsibility that have nothing to do with our home. Much of my working day is spent doing things and seeing people she knows nothing about. As a mature and sane woman, she understands that and fully releases me to my work.

Yet, many Christians live in a mindless assumption that Jesus' interests and responsibilities are confined to the church. We're often like a completely self-absorbed wife; my health, my kitchen, my emotions, my projects just have to be what this marriage is about. We simply cannot imagine that our Husband is even remotely knowledgeable about—let alone that he could be the leader of—all power and authority throughout the whole earth. To us, he is the head (and only a ceremonial one at that) of the Missions Department, the Women's Ministry, Teen Mania, and perhaps the choir. We assume he's interested in the sermon topics, the Easter Pageant, the church's budget, and the number of people who have decided to "accept" him.

This woefully inadequate and impoverished view of him represents a shocking ignorance of the Lord of the whole earth. In fact, the average Christian believer simply does not know him! We do not see the majesty of his reign, the eternal beauty of his character, or the breathtaking and panoramic scope of his capacities. Jesus is the largest Person in all of history. He is the one whom the Father and Creator chose to be the King of the whole thing.

Visitations

You visit the earth and water it, You greatly enrich it; The river of God is full of water; You provide their grain, For so You have prepared it.

> You water its ridges abundantly, You settle its furrows; You make it soft with showers, You bless its growth.
> You crown the year with Your goodness, And Your paths drip with

abundance. They drop on the pastures of the wilderness, And the
little hills rejoice on every side.
The pastures are clothed with flocks; The valleys also are covered
with grain; They shout for joy, they also sing.

PSALMS 65:9-13 NKJV

In this Psalm, God is shown as going round the earth, as a gardener, caring for the land and providing everything the land requires. He continues until the earth is drenched and soaked with a rich supply of refreshment. When he visits, he is attentive to detail. He searches intently, as it all parades before him. He looks for anything that is lacking. When He leaves, the meadows are clothed with flocks, the hills are rejoicing, the valleys are covered with grain. The whole land shouts and sings for joy.

The Hebrew word translated as "visit" in this passage carries a regal significance. It suggests an exacting inspection and even a military parade (as everything passes under his scrutinizing review). Such a visit is a solemn, momentous, even terrifying, occasion. His gaze penetrates right through all methods, materials, and motives. He misses nothing. In the language of Hebrews 4:13, " . . . there is no creature hidden from his sight, but all things are open and laid bare to the eyes of him with whom we have to do."

If we had a more accurate view of his majestic person and office, perhaps we would have a corresponding understanding of the depth and sweep of his visitations. But, we have so shriveled and domesticated our view of him that we tend to see his visitations to the earth as initiated by us! For example, we think of his visitations to earth in terms of "revival" or "renewal" *of the church.* And, of course, he always comes in *response* to the fact that "God's people have humbled themselves and prayed," or that "we agree" that he will come. In other words, he's just sitting in Heaven waiting for us to initiate his visitations. And, of course, those visits will be to his "wife." He is not to go anywhere else.

Apparently, we just don't believe that Jesus, Lord of the whole earth, is capable of understanding the needs of the planet or developing his own work list.

The Mountainous Christ

Spurgeon is not only helpful in once again providing a more realistic view of Jesus, but he is actually quite radical in what he suggests:

> Our knowledge of Christ is somewhat like climbing one of our Welsh mountains. When you are at the base you see but little: the mountain itself appears to be but one-half as high as it really is. Confined in a little valley, you discover scarcely anything but the rippling brooks as they descend into the stream at the foot of the mountain.
>
> Climb the first rising knoll, and the valley lengthens and widens beneath your feet. Go higher, and you see the country for four or five miles round, and you are delighted with the widening prospect. Mount still, and the scene enlarges; till at last, when you are on the summit, and look east, west, north, and south, you see almost all England lying before you. Yonder is a forest in some distant county, perhaps two hundred miles away, and here the sea, and there a shining river and the smoking chimneys of a manufacturing town, or the masts of the ships in a busy port . . .[17]

The far away manufacturing and sea trade are inconceivable to those who remain in the valley and obsessed with the concerns and issues of valley life.

Here's the radical prospect: the higher we go on the mountainous Christ, we discover that the unfolding panorama becomes less "Christian." As we get closer to the summit of the mountain-

---

[17] Charles Spurgeon, *Morning and Evening*, June 24

ous Christ, we see sights and issues—the smoking chimneys of a manufacturing town, or the masts of the ships in a busy port—that have nothing at all to do with our own Christian provincialisms. As the atmosphere begins to clear of earth's (including the church's) contaminants, we start to see clearly His majestic and sweeping reign of the earth.

It is only then that we begin to catch a glimpse of the fact that He—our own Husband—is King of the whole earth!

The real problem with our knowledge of Jesus is that we (Christians and churches) are "confined in a little valley." Because we live out our lives at such a low altitude, we simply have no way to behold the breathtaking grandeur of who he really is. Exacerbating the problem is that our own cultural superstitions warn us to never leave the valley. We've accepted that "it's just too dangerous up there." So, we rarely if ever read a "non-Christian" book, listen to real music, golf or eat with anyone outside our own little circle, or hang out at Starbucks on a Sunday morning. That would just be venturing too far from the valley.

But if we ever do put on hiking gear and head for the high country, we'll be stunned as "the valley lengthens and widens beneath our feet" and we discover whole vistas that we never dreamed of. "Go higher, and you see" the unfurling panorama of his character, his attributes, his intelligence, and his world. You might even catch a glimpse of some of his people; people who look nothing at all like you!

Chapter 8

THE LITTLE CHURCH IN THE VALLEY

The problems of the American church are primarily altitude (not attitude) issues. In general, church folks are fair and decent people. They are not depraved. I've never known them to stomp on puppies.

But, when individuals, families, and their institutions are confined to a narrow little vale tucked away below the mountain ranges, abnormalities take root. First, because the view is so restricted, life in the valley is isolated from the larger rhythms, measures, and disciplines of community. And, that always introduces "special" rules, exemptions, language, and ideas. Consequently, life becomes conforming, superstitious, grossly aberrant, and eventually incestuous. Life outside the valley is impossible to imagine. Life in the valley becomes its own separate and grotesque bubble of reality. You don't understand? Watch the movie "Deliverance."

In such a valley, outsiders are viewed with great suspicion. And, here's the dilemma for the American institution we call the church: Jesus is the ultimate outsider. He came from Heaven to a planet (not a group). Although he lived out the entirety of that life within a microscopic dot on that planet, he never had a group or provincial view. As Lord of the whole earth here on a mission, he saw everything from a very high vantage point. Jesus brought a stunningly eternal and commanding "world view" to his earthly life.

What did Jesus' church look like?

Jesus, the Son of God, the Lord of the whole earth, reached down into the valley of humanity and pulled a few disciples up the mountain into fellowship. That was his church. Read about their normal life activities and conversations. Through him, those guys—simple, hardworking folks—saw and heard mysteries. As incredible as it sounds, these uneducated and uncomplicated men hung out with God! Through him, they learned how to live in a way that saw "heaven on earth." And, because of the continuous availability of Heavenly reality on this plane, healing diseases, evicting evil spirits, conversing with storms, walking around on the water, even raising the dead were all expressions of normal life. They lived so high on the mountain of Christ that some even saw him meeting with the long-dead Elijah and Moses (when Peter blurted out some "valley talk" about a building program).

Consider their conversations. Jesus often pulled that veil back and gave them a view that saints and prophets from other eras had wanted to see (Matthew 13:17). His view of time was supple and fluid; it floated back and forth like a bottle on the sea of eternity. For example, he could show them things about "the end of the age" in the same conversation that gave them a peek at Noah building the ark.

Peter, James, John and his other disciples weren't scholars or theologians or even necessarily devout. But, they were *with him*! And, that was all that was necessary for them to become pregnant with the "incorruptible seed" as Peter so clearly (and probably wistfully) remembered it years later.

If you had photographs of Jesus' church, they would include shots of folks walking down dusty roads, crowds sitting on hillsides, people fishing, and a few disciples gathered around tables with wine and food. Even when he chose "the twelve," the primary purpose of their association was that "they might be with him" (Mark 3:14).

I think simplicity would be the most common distinctive of the photos. Just people with Jesus. If you look closely, you will notice that all of the pictures of him on the earth seem to portray a total independence from the systems, riches, and expectations of earth and a corresponding dependence on his Father in Heaven. Watch his everyday interactions with people. It does not seem to matter to him whether they are male, female, adult, child, rich, poor, devout, unbelieving, Jewish, Roman, or Samaritan. He listens, questions, engages. He seems to give everyone a fair hearing and doesn't try to bring anyone to conclusions. We are seeing real conversations; they are not scripted or agenda-driven. This is pure simplicity of heart.

I've often wondered how he would interact in our day with a person who is a criminal, a Buddhist, an atheist, a homosexual, a grouch, a quadriplegic, mentally impeded, or a militant Muslim? If we were somehow able to watch him in such a contemporary situation (say at Starbucks), I don't believe his conversation with them would even remotely remind us of anyone else we've ever known or seen. I don't believe any words moving across his lips would even resemble any statements we've ever heard from anyone else.

What does today's Church in the Valley look like?

George Barna makes a crucially important point about the church. " . . . *the Bible neither describes nor promotes the local church as we know it today* [italics his] . . . the local church many have come to cherish— the services, offices, programs, buildings, ceremonies—is neither biblical nor unbiblical. It is abiblical—that is, such an organization is not addressed in the Bible."[18]

Perhaps the most distinctive thing about the church in the valley is its isolation from reality. The fact that it is considered an event (defined by a time and place and name) is profoundly bizarre. The church of the Bible is a relationship of love, not a place and not an occurrence. Those very distinctives make today's church quite detached and unrelated to the details and cycles of normal life (there is no evidence at all that Jesus' church met at a regular place or time or had a name). Time and place and group names are all cultural derivations; they are control mechanisms of the old order.

One of the biggest threats to local churches is outsiders, those who are different. Because we live in an ingrown (and incestuous) valley, we "don't take kindly to strangers round here." So, take the same list of people mentioned above in an imagined encounter with Jesus (the criminal, Buddhist, atheist, etc.) and consider typical Christian encounters. When those people appear, our muscles tighten, our eyes divert, and our mind races to remember the cold calculus of methods and agendas. We seem incapable of just relating to people normally. We're not very good at just taking life as it comes.

For example, if a lesbian couple asks for directions to the courthouse, our mind races through many issues. Only one is relevant; do we know where the courthouse is? If someone is intoxicated and asks us for money, we tend to process a myriad of convoluted responses. But, there is only one request on the table: money. Give or don't give and move on with life. A man of Jehovah's Witness faith knocks on our door and asks if he can come in and talk to us. It's only a question; the menu of answers ranges from

---

[18] Barna, *Revolution*, p. 37

"yes" to "no." But, a tangle of debates and objectives block our ability to simply hear and respond.

That's what life in the valley does to attitudes about outsiders.

Photos of the contemporary valley church would reveal that the most prominent and visible feature is *buildings*. In fact, today, the very definition of "church" has been reduced to a building. And, we have Gothic, Renaissance, Greek Revival, modern, shopping center, big ones, little ones, pretty ones, ugly ones. And, of course, acres of parking lots. And inside those buildings, the most visible sights would be the creature comforts (reclining seats, coffee bars, air conditioning, very expensive and complex sound and lighting systems, sophisticated A/V equipment, etc.).

It is fair to conclude that the most compelling difference between the two churches—his and ours—is the very simple centrality issue; his church was about him and ours is about us. An e-newsletter from *LeadershipJournal.net* carried an article by a Pastor named Ron Benson about his attempts to flow with new worship forms. It captures a funny and disturbing view of the post-Jesus church:

> I tried the Journaling Station. I sat on the little stool with an orange crayon in my hand and a blank place on the paper tablecloth in front of me. I scribbled a little, making crosses. I made three crosses. I made three crosses on a little hill. I put three little "V" shapes in the corner for birds. I wanted to be inspired and inspiring. I wanted to be enraptured with artistic worship. I wanted to be filled to overflowing with creative juices.
>
> *Maybe that's it*, I thought. So I meandered over to the Creative Juices Bar and whispered an order for a raw mango and pineapple. Some chanting started, a kind of repeating the first line of Leviticus 18, "Say this to your people, 'I am the Lord, the Lord your God.'"

I wondered if they'd be getting into further exegesis of the chapter when a conga-line came by and swept me up.[19]

That little vignette is almost enough by itself to tell reasonably intelligent people that Jesus has blown the building.

How did Jesus and his church relate to money?

No area is more revealing of the great chasm between Jesus' church and the Church in the Valley than attitudes toward money and possessions. One reflects a dependence on God; the other reveals a frantic sense of self (which, naturally, must march under a banner of religious language). Even though he talked a great deal about money, the scriptures portray Jesus as somewhat detached from, perhaps even dismissive of, money and possessions. For example, there's no record that he ever asked for or received an offering. Jesus' economic attitude is well summarized in Matthew 6:19 - 34:

> Do not store up for yourselves treasures on earth, where moth and rust destroy, and where thieves break in and steal. But store up for yourselves treasures in heaven, where moth and rust do not destroy, and where thieves do not break in and steal. For where your treasure is, there your heart will be also.
>
> . . . No one can serve two masters. Either he will hate the one and love the other, or he will be devoted to the one and despise the other. You cannot serve both God and Money. Therefore I tell you, do not worry about your life, what you will eat or drink; or about your body, what you will wear. Is not life more important than food, and the body more important than clothes?
>
> Look at the birds of the air; they do not sow or reap or store away in barns, and yet your heavenly Father feeds them. Are you not much more valuable than they?

---

[19] Ron Benson, LeadershipJournal.net, August 10, 2004 http://www.christianitytoday.com/leaders/newsletter/2004/cln40810.html

. . . do not worry, saying, 'What shall we eat?' or 'What shall we drink?' or 'What shall we wear?' For the pagans run after all these things, and your heavenly Father knows that you need them. But seek first his kingdom and his righteousness, and all these things will be given to you as well.

Tragically, the simplicity and trust captured in these words of Jesus are totally foreign concepts to contemporary Christians. To actually live like that would be viewed today as unrealistic, crazy, and downright dangerous.

How does the Church in the Valley relate to money?

In the beginning, God gave specific economic policies in his constitution for his new nation, Israel. In all that he said about the poor, property, fraud, usury, etc., it is clear that he retains the ownership of everything[20] (apparently, he intends that his created beings should go to him with their needs). His order was righteous, just, and established a peaceful and generous habitation.

Years later, when Israel rejected God's benevolent leadership and asked for a king, the result was the exact opposite of his realm. The new and very human leadership merchandised the people. They were severely oppressed and exploited (I Samuel 8:11-19). Before long, many were "in distress, in debt, discontented," and looking for God's idea of leadership again (I Samuel 22:2). In God's economy, he provides money and other resources to his children. It is a simple relationship issue. He, the Owner of all, is our father. In the course of our daily walk with him, he provides all the support we need for our earthly sustenance.

---

[20] For example, he decreed that land could not be permanently owned, debt had to be retired every seven years, and slaves and land were to be set free every fifty years.

However, in the systems of the world, money is a master. It seduces people with, and enslaves them to, an illusory assurance of freedom and power. But, the freedom it promises is an appeal to our hereditary rebellion against Father. Perversely, it seems that however long we have known him, we are easily and quickly tantalized by the possibility that we might be free of him. For some reason, we long to be self-sufficient and unrestrained.

Money says it will help.

And, the power which money promises to us will inevitably involve human slavery. Think of it: the raw imagery of power—sexual extravagance, financial domination, unlimited leisure, more and nicer possessions—almost always requires the loss, humiliation, or even blood of others.

There is no area where the church has become more conformed to—*pressed into the mold of*—the world than in financial issues. And, sadly, most church and Christian organization leaders are content to *leave* those financial assumptions wholly within the realm of the unexamined. In my own consulting work with churches and organizations, I've seen that a shortage of funds nearly always produces a grab for new marketing strategies, pressure tactics ("time to preach on tithes and offerings" or calling "the partners," or raising a special offering), efforts to increase volunteers while firing staff, etc. There are also parallel assumptions about the need for better and bigger buildings, later and greater technologies, and health care and retirement programs.

The televangelist scandals, the new sophistication of ministry fundraising, and the acquisition of political power by the church are merely the tip of the iceberg of the church's outright and unexamined acceptance of the "money as master" philosophy.

How does the Church in the Valley consider the poor?

The real problem of poverty is not a shortage of cash. The issue is not about taking a cruise or buying an i-Pod. The real problem is *powerlessness*. It strips people of control and dignity and leaves them with no power base from which to negotiate the demands and perplexities of life.

The powerful often criticize the poor for "whining"; that's just a rich guy's spin on "pleading" for mercy. Because they have no power source, the poor cannot successfully battle with banks or utility companies. Nor can they demand that the rich pay up. The realities of life have molded them into a pleading posture.

When the church embraces an economic view which sees relationships as profit-based, then those who have more money will have more value. The poor will inevitably be devalued. I think that must be why James wrote:

> Suppose a man comes into your meeting wearing a gold ring and fine clothes, and a poor man in shabby clothes also comes in. If you show special attention to the man wearing fine clothes and say, "Here's a good seat for you," but say to the poor man, "You stand there or sit on the floor by my feet," have you not discriminated among yourselves and become judges with evil thoughts?
>
> Listen, my dear brothers: Has not God chosen those who are poor in the eyes of the world to be rich in faith and to inherit the kingdom he promised those who love him? But you have insulted the poor . . . James 2:2-6 NIV

The pastor of a large suburban church near my home freely admits that he is "called to the rich." It is, after all, the smart ministry marketing decision.

How does God view the poor?

This passage may contain the seed of understanding of God's view of the poor:

> Then Jesus said to his host, "When you give a luncheon or dinner, do not invite your friends, your brothers or relatives, or your rich neighbors; if you do, they may invite you back and so you will be repaid.
>
> But when you give a banquet, invite the poor, the crippled, the lame, the blind, and you will be blessed. Although they cannot repay you, you will be repaid at the resurrection of the righteous." Luke 14:12-14 (NIV)

Is it possible that Jesus was revealing a great secret here? Was He saying that we can invest in something here and now that will produce an eternal return? Perhaps by their very inability to participate in a market-based economy, the poor have greater value—a head start—in the real economy. Could it be that, if we humble ourselves, we'll find that the poor have the unique authority and capacity to pull us up to the economy of God's Kingdom?

If so, part of the reason may be the relational issue. The ones who should not be invited are all self-sufficient. They need nothing. Conversely, those at the top of Jesus' invitation list all have serious needs. They cannot even get into the banquet without help. Yet, they have access to something which the host cannot get without *their* help: eternal prosperity. Is Jesus suggesting that our earth views of one another are too limited by class consciousness?

Is he once again transcending the arthritic rational of the old era with the larger view that—just as the body parts are interrelated without regard for "beauty" and honor—that we all have need of one another, regardless of limitations and weaknesses?

Leadership

Leaders lead. The whole idea of leadership accepts that wisdom and knowledge reside in one and that others recognize and embrace that mysterious reality. So, naturally, the idea of leadership also assumes the freedom to go and the freedom to follow.

So, what if Jesus, the Good Shepherd, decided to lead his flock away from the Church of the Valley onto an ascending path up the mountain? Would we even know that? How could we respond? We can't just leave. We have salaries to pay, a mortgage to cover, programs to sustain, personal expectations to satisfy, and goals to meet. Additionally, our website, our newspaper ads, and our other marketing tools have committed us to be at a time and place.

The Bible speaks of Jesus as being "lifted up." If you read even a little of the Gospels, you quickly see that in His "local church," His elevation was a natural and simple reality; that church was all about Him. It was not about a place, a time, nor a name. It was just people with Jesus. They were continually looking up to him (as sheep would naturally "look up"). After all, He was the Leader, the Center, the Reason, and the Initiator of their life together. He alone had life. Their chief role was to *receive* that life. There is no indicator that when he was not with them, they went ahead and met anyway.

One of the most persistent features of the American church is its continual rumbling roar; the activities, programs, and events never stop. I've personally seen church leaders break down and become hospitalized because of that incessant roar. And, we all know the toll of that relentless pace on individuals, marriages, and family life. Many are helplessly caught under the track of a religious juggernaut which climbs right up their back and leaves a trail of broken lives in its wake.

So, are we to assume that the Good Shepherd doesn't lead his flock to rest and never leads them beyond what they already know?

How can any honest and objective assessment of the American church escape the very same observation that Jesus had in His day, "When he saw the crowds, he had compassion on them, because they were harassed and helpless, like sheep without a shepherd." (Matthew 9:36 NIV).

It is an inescapable and appalling truth: the Church in the Valley does not have a shepherd. The leader is Me.

Chapter 9

SMOG IN THE VALLEY

The US Environmental Protection Agency defines smog as "a mixture of pollutants, principally ground-level ozone, produced by chemical reactions in the air involving smog-forming chemicals. A major portion of smog-formers come from burning of petroleum-based fuels such as gasoline. Other sources, volatile organic compounds, are found in products such as paints and solvents." [21]

In other words smog is the evidence of man, the congested choking residue of what was surely our "best and brightest." It all looked so good on paper, gurgling in the laboratory, screaming around the test track, or discussed in the focus group. How could it miss? How could it harm?

But, years later, we and the environment are drowning in that polluting swirl of choking, burning, killing air.

Naturally, where there are concentrations of people, there are matching densities of pollution. Many people live in an unthinking assumption that pollution is only an environmental issue. But, "smog" also has an intellectual, spiritual, and cultural dimension. It seems that the Apostle Paul's lament is true, not only at a personal level, but on a broad, societal basis: "O wretched man that I am! Who will deliver me from this body of death?" (Romans 7:24 NKJV)

We cannot escape the stench, the toxicity, the wretched effects of . . . us. It is, of course, the low elevations that suffer the greatest contamination. In fact, The Living Bible has an interesting

---

[21] http://oaspub.epa.gov

translation of Romans 7:24—"Oh what a terrible predicament I'm in! *Who will free me from my slavery to this deadly lower nature?*" The lower elevations of anything—air, religion, entertainment, philosophy, etc.—are more enslaving and deadly than the higher elevations. Those on the political left in America prefer to focus on one kind of cultural or political contamination; those on the right are disposed toward another. But, there's no real difference. It's all part of the smog which chokes the valley.

As the church has descended into more of an earthbound position, it has come down the mountain away from the simplicity in Christ. Consequently, it has become increasingly poisoned by the smog that chokes the valley. Part of the reason that Jesus has disappeared is a simple matter of elevations—as the church has dropped to the valley floor, it has become more separated from him and more trapped in a human-designed and polluted atmosphere. After breathing poison air and drinking toxic water for a while, living organisms become accustomed to contamination. They don't even realize they are swallowing death. That is the condition of the contemporary American church.

The Smog of Sensuality

Most of us think of sensuality in terms of the erotic. But, a sensuous life is simply one that is lived according to the senses. It is a life in tilt away from the spiritual part of our composition toward the urges and cravings that reside within our physical body.

Yes, God made our sensate dimensions and they are to be enjoyed. It seems to me that the significant and the sensual are essential *and* polar opposites. In other words, maybe they are like contrasting pulls of a muscle.

However, at the risk of sounding Gnostic, I wonder if the more sensual we are, the less we know of true significance. Significance rises like cream. Inevitably, that pulls away from the lower regions of our "basic instinct." Few of us realize the extent to which we are cashing in significance for sensuousness. We are often like Esau, trading the timeless value of our eternal birthright for the "pottage" of immediate gratification of our senses.

The sensual vs. significant contest plays out in so many ways. Humanity's best and brightest efforts always run toward the sensual. "There is a way that seems right to a man, But its end is the way of death." (Proverbs 14:12 NKJV). The intuitions buried in the "seems right" will always veer away from what is truly important or valuable. We are necessarily like a car out of alignment; we always favor the ditch of sensuality. Our economy, social structure, public policy matrix, moral frameworks, technologies, and even our theologies all converge to produce results which are more alluring than they are valuable.

Micro-managing life

The first thing that hits me at 4:30 a.m. is not a yearning for God but a full-blown, full-body press into the presence of . . . coffee. I stumble to the dark kitchen and push the button that delivers that steaming hot black-as-Pennzoil stuff into that carafe. Oh, the first sip of that rich and aromatic rush! It not only pulls coffee beans into my system, waking me to new and vibrant possibilities, but more important, brings a surging confidence that all is well with the world, the future, and the relations between God and man. But, it takes me about an hour of drugging out on caffeine before I'm ready to talk to God or man.

Hours later, Joanne curls into her chair by the fireplace, taking slow and romantic pulls from the cup. The drug achieves the same beautiful thing for her, but she's much more serene and sociable about it.

When we travel, our coffee addictions take different forms. We just get on the road and find the first . . . Starbucks. We can spot that round green lighted logo up to six miles away through a heavy fog and in a rolling sea of other neon signs. We've probably been to half the Starbucks in America. When we walk in, Judy or Tim or Juan calls us by name. I think they must have our photos and dossiers behind the counter.

I am not making this up: on a recent trip, we drove two-hundred and ten miles—about fifty of those miles with caffeine headaches of increasing severity—without coffee of any kind because we didn't see a Starbucks! We were finally cell phoning friends and family, pleading with them to go online and find the Starbucks nearest to our journey. Things got ugly. Heaven was silent. Despair settled over the land.

Finally, in desperation and shame, we careened our van into a McDonald's. The screech of tires braking on the asphalt. I ran inside and pounded on the steel counter: "I want two cups of coffee and I want them RIGHT NOW!" Others standing in the serving lines apparently decided to go elsewhere for breakfast. *He might have a gun.*

Later, as my savage heart purred in caffeinated contentment, I watched the farms and forests and towns and trailer parks flowing past our van. Joanne was asleep. Emmylou Harris provided the soundtrack as I began to wonder when and how brand loyalty took over and conquered the quiet rhythms of life. I finally and sorrowfully had to conclude that it all flows from my compulsion to micro-manage my life. I leave nothing to caprice (or God). I must control it.

Whatever happened to taking life as it comes?

As I drove, the ephemeral whisper of old memories began to drift into my mind. *At twelve years old, I and my nine-year-old brother Vernon are working with Dad, loading trash in the pickup. The blazing sun of the August sky turns all of South Central Kansas into an oven. We all climb into the sawdust-and-sweat scented cab of the pickup for the choking dusty drive to the city dump. And, Dad, wiping perspiration from his forehead, says, "Boys, you wanna cold drink?"*

Those words, rarely spoken by our Great Depression-shaped and very frugal father, were as musical as ice-cubes tumbling into a tall crystal goblet. They always pulled me into a mysterious realm of anticipated cold relief and a moment of sweet communion with Dad. Standing there in the service bay of the Pratt Co-Op station, holding that *so-cold-it-hurt* Orange Crush or Royal Crown Cola or whatever to my lips was a moment suspended between heaven and earth.

Such a glowing moment was produced by a serendipitous impulse, a relationship-infused stretch for something. It was a wholly spontaneous time which arrived in Dad's mind as a part of taking life as it comes. Those moments were steeped in a significance which touched the traces of our familial identity.

Taking life as it comes is rare these days.

Visualize this scene: you're driving along a mountain highway, you glide around the bend at twilight and there you see a little log-constructed café nestled in a cove of towering pines. Blue smoke is floating up out of the stone chimney. You realize "my gosh, I'm hungry," and pull in for a "bite of supper."

For too many of us, those little peaks of whimsy never happen anymore. Why? Marketing has become the so intense and pervasive that we've been tweaked into a screaming turbo-charged devotion to brands. We can't just glide onto that little café in the mountains because we're going to drive till we find Chili's or Applebee's or Wendy's. We *can't* even pull off for a generic cup of coffee, because anything less than Starbucks just means settling for less than the best. And not only do we "deserve" the best that man has to offer, but we live in a consumer economy that will deliver it to us.

The Market View of the World

The science of marketing, like any discipline or paradigm, is primarily a way of viewing reality. It looks at an objective truth through the lens of a very specific and calculated purpose. And, when marketing looks at people, it sees "customers." It's not wrong; it's simply a way of seeing. Of course, that way of seeing has strategic value for the economy.

Philip Kotler, the famous Professor of International Marketing at the Northwestern University Kellogg Graduate School of Management in Chicago, is (according to his own "Kotler Marketing Group" website) "the author of many - if not most - of the leading books in the field of marketing management." Consider how Kotler describes that way of seeing:

> "The marketplace is . . . a jungle. Marketers have to scope out the jungle (market research) and define the prey that they want to capture (target marketing). Marketers must study the prey's habits and habitats (consumer behavior). Marketers have to build a better mousetrap (product differentiation), lay traps and bait (advertising, direct mail, sales promotions), and secure the prey and prevent it from escaping (customer retention, relationship marketing).

The hunters/marketers assume that the prey is not as smart or well informed as they are. The prey acts on emotion (positioning), is easily seduced by trinkets (promotions), and wanders unwittingly into the danger zone (retail stores, salespeople). The hunter has extensive information about the whereabouts of the prey, and knows how to aim the rifle (value proposition) at the prey's soft spot.[22]

That way of seeing people may be essential as a driver for our economy, but it is one of the primary pollutants which contribute to the smog in the little valley where the church exists. It reduces people down to simple economic units. In doing so, it often tramples "the hopes and fears of all the years" in the stampede to find and develop customers.

Here's the crux of the problem: the market simply cannot *see* into the profound mysteries which God has layered into human vessels. Therefore, the market drive always threatens to trample people. The market exploits and violates human vulnerabilities. Furthermore, it carries a hostility to God's gracious leadership and generous provision.

Those who think of themselves as Godly leaders should be more vigilant in protecting people from the market. That's because the marketplace has a remarkable ignorance of the whole idea of sacred space; those who merchandise simply fail to recognize or respect other realms (such as the environment, the family, local schools or churches). "The market" assumes sovereignty. That was probably the issue in why Jesus drove the merchants from the temple (John 2:13-17). He was violently disrupting the infusion of marketing into the sacred space of the temple. In so doing, He was also challenging the economy, the social structure, the moral constructs, and the theologies which insisted on choosing man's

[22] Philip Kotler, *Kellogg on Marketing* (New York: John Wiley & Sons, 2001) p. 387

best and brightest over God's sovereign and gracious leadership.

The modern market has achieved an unprecedented level of precision and sophistication. And, that has permeated right through the walls and windows of the church. Today, it is assumed by many that the church *is* a business—that it is by design compatible with the same principles and attitudes which drive enterprise. Walk into any Christian bookstore and look at the titles. You will see a church-business syncretism that should disturb and offend. Incredibly, it doesn't. We're too adjusted to the smog.

The ironic result of the business-church osmosis is that pastors (ostensibly the very shepherds who are ready to die to protect the sheep) have rolled over. Too many have embraced this view—a view which ruthlessly exposes and merchandises the sheep—and have incorporated it into church life.

Whatever happened to worship?

Perhaps no area is a better laboratory for testing and understanding the "sensual vs. significance" contest than our worship.

Let's start at the simplest and purest origins of worship: the fact that we walk upright gives an important clue about our nature. Like trees, we are always in an ascension posture; it is natural for us to look up. We are cathedrals.

Today, we live in such a manufactured environment—climate-controlled, artificially-lit, technology-rich space—that it's easy to lose sight of our primitive orientation to the universe.

I was recently recalibrated to that relationship when I crossed the Pacific from Honolulu to San Diego on an aircraft carrier. From the 3 a.m. total darkness of the ship's fantail, with salty air in my nostrils, I gazed up at through an uncommonly clear night sky. And there, I was transfixed by the rarely seen brilliance of diamonds-on-black-velvet stars. That moment reconnected me to a basic truth: when we live in umbilical connection to the natural environment, we cannot help but be invaded by the spiritual dimension. We must stand in awe of the creation and the Creator. In that awareness, it is instinctive for the eyes to widen, the heart to be quickened, the mouth to fall open, and hands to go up. That's called "worship."

But, because of our manufactured habitats, we cannot even think of worship in its simple and pristine reality. Today, "worship" means a music genre, an event, and a marketing angle.

Think of David under the stars, declaring his adoration to Someone up there in the dark.

In a very short distance from that, I have often walked into a room with ten or more people. We were there "groping for God." No one had a musical instrument. We had no "worship leader," no sound system, nothing to clutter the transport of heart to Heaven. In fact, no one was even thinking of music. All we were thinking was . . . God! The how, the what, the where were irrelevant; God would provide all of that. The only thing he was looking for was hearts that were completely his. That was it.

That is still it! And, when he finds them, nothing else is needed and nothing else is allowed.

Os Guinness has captured the "significance vs. sensuousness" dichotomy very well; he wistfully recalls:

> "…moments in public worship when it was as if the ceiling was punctured and there was an eruption of the transcendent . . .
>
> Sometimes the irruption happened during the hymns, sometimes during the preaching, and sometimes during the Holy Communion. It was certainly nothing that was engineered. But it was deep, real, transfixing, and the light it cast would throw the week behind and the week ahead into a different light. "Did those who lead the worship pray and expect such a breaking-in of the

supernatural in ways we no longer do, even with our improved stage management, our choreography, our dance, our drama, and our PowerPoint expositions? When was the last time the ceiling was punctured in your local worship? [23]

Nothing in all our biography could be more significant than our communion with God. But, incredibly, we invited sensuality to the meeting. And, it has contaminated and complicated the simplicity of our worship.

How did sensuality get into worship?

I have seen and heard it many times; we were standing in that "groping-for-God" moment. We knew nothing; we had nothing. We were just reaching out for him. Sometimes when his Spirit moved into that room of humans, a *sound* began to stir. The sound originated somewhere else and was, indeed, unearthly. It was *almost* like wind. Then, it sometimes took on a chime-like tinkling. As it began to increase, voices were pulled out of the assembled human vessels and became part of the swirling wind and chimes; the sounds of Heaven were energizing and blending with sounds from the earth. That integration was profoundly moving and mesmerizing. Then, the sound often became musical in the same sense that a river spilling over and rocks can be heard as *almost* singing.

Very often that musical nature of worship swelled into a powerful flow that was composed and harmonic. I've stood in such moments and listened as that sound carried the thunderous majesty of a great waterfall. And, sometimes it found sounds never heard before and sometimes it picked up recognizable human songs. You've never heard "The Love of God" or "It is Well with My Soul" or "To God be the Glory" till you've heard them

---

[23] Os Guinness, *Prophetic Untimeliness* (Grand Rapids, MI: Baker Books, 2003) p 111

Footprints in the Sea

groaned out in these Heaven-kissing-earth moments. In such times, I've wondered if my heart would be pulled from my chest.

And, then, somewhere, sometime, someone had the good idea to support this sound with a piano or maybe it was a Hammond B3 or a saxophone. Then, genuinely stirred, other musicians looked at each other, nodded, and quietly started unpacking their Fender Stratocasters, the drum sets, and the bass guitars. Now, of course, they needed amplifiers and, yes, a sound system. Not too much— "don't want to take away from the Spirit"—but enough so that the worshipers can find the right keys and rhythms for what is tumbling from their heaving chests. After all, God is a God of order.

The good idea was now rolling like a proverbial snowball down a mountain side.

Before long, someone recorded the sound; you know, so that others could join in the worship. Then, technology heard the sounds; it raised it head, its ears stood up and tuned toward the music flowing from the meetings. Companies were formed, marketing deals struck, and soon the "Praise and Worship" sound was hitting the 3:00 a.m. television infomercial world and even Wall Street. Songwriters and "worship leaders" were soaring.

But, man wasn't through. His good ideas were now bubbling like a cauldron of stew on high heat. Concerts were produced; killer sound and lighting systems created, and corporate sponsors were waiving money and screaming like traders on the floor of stock exchanges.

Into this sensory-overload came a new breed of worship artists. They had record deals and agents and managers and accountants and they had great funk and grunge clothing. They stood on stages, amidst the swirling colored lasers, raging synthesizers, and led the waving seas of outstretched arms into Jesus lyrics. Was it purely coincidental that the women worship artists were unfailingly beautiful, trim, and kinda sexy? Apparently, average women do not worship.

Of course, all this happened through the presentation of the very best that man has to offer. He was just trying to help.

The sensuality factor triumphed. And, Jesus disappeared again.[24]

So, what do we do about the smog problem?

The sensory dimensions of valley life will always pull worship or anything else into a vortex around us.

But, smog is not the real problem. It is simply a condition of life down in the valley. It would be foolish to challenge the smog. The only real choice we have is to move on up the mountain of Christ. Simply turn away and "look unto the hills from when comes our help." Leave the complex, contaminated, noxiously sensual atmosphere of the lower regions behind.

For example, those who attend musical concerts will notice that what happens in "worship" concerts looks, sounds, and feels almost identical to an Alan Jackson or Janet Jackson concert. It is an inevitable result of living in the valley. It is not strange and it is not going to change. It is futile to react.

One can only move to higher elevations.

---

[24] Of course, I quickly admit that he sometimes appears in these sensory-overload productions (a.k.a. "concerts"). He is the Lord and he can appear anywhere, anytime he chooses.

Chapter 10

A Simple Altar

I wonder why the Bible records that God gave such detailed directions on the construction of altars. According to Exodus 20:24-25, God said:

> The altars you make for me must be simple altars of earth. Offer upon them your sacrifices to me-your burnt offerings and peace offerings of sheep and oxen. Build altars only where I tell you to, and I will come and bless you there.
>
> You may also build altars from stone, but if you do, then use only uncut stones and boulders. Don't chip or shape the stones with a tool, for that would make them unfit for my altar.

Apparently, an altar is a place to die. It is not a work of art. An altar made of the earth's raw stuff was sufficient and perfect. Engraving or craftsmanship of any kind would profane it.

One of the most difficult things for us to understand is that God is, all by himself, enough. We think he can be improved. There is something in our nature that wants to help, to make it better, to use our skills (which are so impressive to us) to do something which will dress up, refine, and improve the natural state. Most of us live our lives around an assumption that man is quite splendid and that God really needs our vast and impressive skills to be brought to the process.

The Seduction of Craft and Complexity

Paul shot straight with the Corinthians: "I am afraid, lest as the serpent deceived Eve by his craftiness, your minds should be led astray from the simplicity and purity of devotion to Christ." (2 Corinthians 11:3 NASB)

The word translated "craftiness" in that verse implies shrewdness, cunning, craft, art. So, Paul, a true shepherd, warned that the tempter could and would use cunning, art, and complexity to pull them away from a simple reliance on the God Who all by Himself is enough.

Charles Simpson once said "there are no holy places; the whole earth is a holy place." But, God's sufficiency (in himself and in his creation) is offensive to our nature. We really want to use our tools. We so want to help, but by doing so, we inevitably corrupt simplicity. When we take our tools to the altars, we get into the business of building holy places (cathedrals, shrines, temples, mosques, etc.).

The process flows something like this:

City parks, hillsides, living rooms, hotel ballrooms, stadiums, or Starbucks are simple, appropriate and sufficient gathering places for any group. Christians who wish to meet (however regularly or irregularly) for purposes of worship, fellowship, inspiration, ceremony, etc. do not carry special meeting needs.

Eventually, however, our desire to be with our own kind (fear of contamination?) and our desire for comfort begin to fabricate thoughts and theologies which support the construction of a special purpose building. Inevitably, we must think of it as holy. Because it is viewed as sacred space, the "church people" go through a subtle shift of identity away from God and to the building.

The construction, furnishing, and maintenance of that building require dollars. So, funding is pulled away from other projects and purposes as "an investment in the future." The rationale, whether explicit or implicit, is that the building will draw more people. Thereby, the building will presumably pay for itself and draw even more money for ministry. "We'll be able to advance the kingdom."

In order to attract the right kind of people, the church hires professionals who will enhance the weekly experience for every member of the family. However, the Executive Pastor first convinces the staff members that ministry is really a labor of love, a privilege, and an honor of service to our Lord. In addition, he tells them, "You know this is a sowing season. And, when the reaping season arrives, we will remember those who labored so faithfully among us." The staff members understand and accept the small salaries.

This process slowly (or sometimes quickly) seduces the people away from the serious pursuit of God and redemptive living. Just like the dynamics of adultery, the flesh-tantalizing creature comforts begin pulling people away from their pure devotion. The Sunday morning event and the building are becoming synonyms for "church." They are inexorably sucking real life out of those who sit and stare from the velvety ergonomic pews. And, the pastor and other staff must find a way to perpetuate the seduction. Like a mistress, the building is demanding more attention, time, respect, and money.

Then, just as an adulterous man may one day awaken and realize this is no good, people start coming to their senses and facing the reality that this is not the "Heaven on earth," mission-focused, worshiping, family-enriching, pure and simple fellowship arrangement they once envisioned or had. So, they start drifting away. Some are burned out. Some seek out alternative or new age formats of spiritual life. Some go fishing. The pastor hates those growing empty spots in the sanctuary.

Money gets tight. The giving to foreign missions decreases. Community-oriented projects are curtailed. Maintenance of the building and the grounds decline, bill payment creeps past 30 days, the underpaid staff members are finally laid off. The pastor begins to regularly remind those who are left that "the people will volunteer freely in the day of his power. . ." Tempers get short, blame is leveled. The Holy Spirit leads the pastor to another church.

Over the years, when the older members bump into each other at soccer games, weddings, or funerals, they always end up talking about the "good old days."

"You know, I'll never forget the time we all roofed that widow's house; you remember we had so many men up on that roof that we had a traffic jam of cars stopping to watch?"

"Oh, and remember that night when we ran into each other at Sears and stood talking in the tool section till they closed and made us leave?"

But, no one ever talks about that damned building or its killer sound system, coffee bar, wedding chapel, or its covered parking.[25]

Walter Wink has written that ". . . every business, corporation, school, denomination, bureaucracy, sports team—indeed, social reality in all its forms—is a combination of both visible and invisible, outer and inner, physical and spiritual. Right at the heart of the most materialistic institutions in society we find spirit."[26]

In the same way, buildings have spirit. They are not benign; they are not neutral designs and constructions. I wonder if the spirit of a building demands obeisance. Is a "holy" building defiant of the Creator?

---

[25] I thank my friend, Mike Bishop, for helping me to think through and articulate this process.

[26] Walter Wink, "The Spirits of Institutions," an essay reprinted from his book, *Engaging the Powers*, in *The Hidden Spirit* (Matthews, NC, Christian Ministry Resources, 1999) p. 18

The Arrogance of Church Buildings

When Solomon prepared to build the temple, he made a grand speech kicking off the project.

"Behold, I am about to build a house for the Lord . . . And the house which I am about to build will be great; for greater is our God than all the gods . . ." (II Chronicles 2: 4-5 NASB).

Then he made a total diversion, a stunning hairpin curve, in his comments:

"But who is able to build a house for Him, for the heavens and the highest heavens cannot contain Him? So who am I, that I should build a house for Him . . . ?" (verse 6)

One can imagine him standing on that grand platform with dignitaries and thousands of workers before him. He begins with the usual yada-yada-yada required at these things. Then, perhaps gazing off into the sky, he seems to have had a bracing reality check, perhaps even an out-of-body experience. At that moment, it seems that his attitude and the content of his speech changed dramatically. In the very next line, verse 6, he said (Chinn version): "Wait a minute; what are we doing? What the hell makes us think that we can or should build a house for God? I mean, the heavens can't contain him. So who am I, that I should try to build a house for him?"

Of course, he went ahead and built it. But, he clearly knew that this thing was for man, not God.

Years later, when Paul stood up in the Areopagus to reason with the very cosmopolitan crowd, he started with the largest issue he could invoke: "The God who made the world and all things in it, since He is Lord of heaven and earth, does not dwell in temples made with hands." (Acts 17:24 NASB)

Perhaps it's significant that the great God-man encounters of the Bible and throughout history did not take place in temples. Yet, many live out an assumption that "church" is the only (or at least primary) place for true encounters with the Lord.

Religious structures exist for humans, not God. Furthermore, most churches stand as symbols of man's arrogance. Christian culture has blinded us to the true outrageousness, intrusiveness, and defiance that a modern church building represents.

Does it mean anything at all to us that God viewed his finished creation and pronounced it "good?" Is it even remotely possible that he meant for us to accept it on the same terms? Did He mean for us to recognize his craftsmanship as being holy? Or, do we need to improve his workmanship by creating "special" buildings as holy places?

Is that why we bulldoze his trees, violently disrupt his intricate ecosystems, and take money from his people in order to build gleaming monuments to our own importance and for our own comfort?

Perhaps worse, church buildings also commemorate, even exalt, our quarrelsome divisions. One idea that seemed important to Paul as he spoke that day in Athens was: "He made from one, every nation of humanity." So, shouldn't people who walk the earth as God's emissaries do all possible to reinforce and honor the created commonality and relational unity of man? Instead, we (Christians) go to great expense, environmental injury, and community insult to build these things that remind the whole world that we can't stand each other.

And, no, it's not enough to build "community considerate" or "environmentally friendly" buildings. These contrived rationales only serve to enable our announcements to God that His creation is not good enough for us. They also give us cover for our "Rhett Butler" confession: "frankly, my dear earth and community, we don't give a damn."

What is it about names?

It could be argued that man is, by the empowerment and authorization of his Creator, a namer. God brought every animal (birds and beasts) to Adam to see what the man would call them. And, the names Adam gave them were honored by God and apparently certified by society and science.

When a name is assigned, something is conferred. A nature, even sometimes a destiny. The name carries an ordination. In so many cases, the named person or thing actually begins to change into conformity with the assignment. That's why as humans, we only have the right to assign names according to our authorization and within our own sphere of responsibility. In other words, because of that impartation of an intangible something, I can give names to my children, my artistic works, or other entities within my authorized domain. But, I cannot name your children, your autobiography, your pets, or your sailboat.

Could it be significant that we find no church names in the Bible?

No geography, theology, or leader-related designations for a local church. None. Bible scholar William Barclay commented about the line in I Corinthians 1:2 which refers to "the church of God which is at Corinth."

"It was not The Church of Corinth; it was the Church of God. To Paul, wherever an individual congregation might be, it was a part of the one Church of God. He would not have spoken of the Church of Scotland or the Church of England; he would not have given the Church a local designation . . ."[27]

---

[27] William Barclay, *The Letters to the Corinthians* (Philadelphia: The Westminister Press, 1975) p. 9

There is simply no record that anyone in "the New Testament church" ever used a name to specify a particular gathering or experience of a local church. In fact, the 16th chapter of Romans records Paul's greeting to five house-churches, but not once did he use an official or institutional name.

Is it possible that our insistence on naming churches is more the result of "valley smog" than it is of any divine authorization? Could it be that "the church of God which [happened to be] at Corinth" may have been more reflective of God's glory than the ones in our day? By naming a local church (or denomination) are we defying The Name That is Above Every Other Name? Should we simply be gathered into His Name rather than institutionalizing (controlling?) what is ostensibly his gathering?

What? A church with no name? How could you "go" to a church that didn't have a name? How would you advertise it? What would you put on the sign out front? What would you write in the Pay-to-the-order-of line of tithe and offering checks? How would you even think of it? What language symbol would the mind grab when planning church-related activities?

No, I am not saying and do not believe that naming a local church is wrong.

But, think about it: a local church is a gathering of hearts under the Lordship of Jesus. He is in charge. It's about him. I think it's possible that all of that begins to erode when a name is assigned. Consider the process:

The Story of Tuesday Night Group

Richard Mash and TD Wellington met in a golf pro shop on a warm Sunday morning in August. They were both looking at the same putter. They ended up talking and wandered over around the "CLOSED" sign to sit in the empty bar. Two hours later, they were exploring careers, marriages, and hollow places of the heart. Three hours later, driving in opposite directions home, both men marveled at the "safe place" they felt with the other. Their stories were told at two dinner time conversations, seven miles apart, with Debra and Jan. Richard and TD were amazed; some eternal itch was being scratched.

From there it wasn't very far to: "Let's invite them over for Labor Day . . . we'll grill some steaks; I'll get some Corona."

In October, a terrible car wreck claimed the life of Richard's Dad and seriously injured Richard and Debra's son, "Spider." They—grandfather and grandson—were on the way home from a football game when they were hit head-on by a delivery truck that had a sudden left front blowout. The Wellingtons were the first friends to arrive at the ER. They embraced Richard and Debra and cried with them.

Then, in a moment which became historic, out of their grief and desperation right there in the hospital waiting room, the two couples began to "seek God, if perhaps they might grope for Him and find Him, though He is not far from each one of us . . ." (Acts 17:27) They found him!

By Christmas, something significant had clearly happened; the two couples were meeting together weekly.   It was the main thing they looked forward to each week—the meal, the wine, the conversation, the prayer time around Spider's rehab bed, the passionate searching of the scriptures. The long recovery time for a thirteen-year-old boy with a spinal cord injury turned into a long period of "groping for God."

The Spirit was brooding over emerging life. Green shoots were breaking the soil of human hearts. Bibles were becoming *alive*; everyday conversations echoed through the corridors of the "eternity in their hearts" (Ecclesiastes 3:11). It was a timeless pattern: tragedy and grief had blown people out of their sedated and satiated routines. Almost magically, others were drawn to the flame of real life which burned in them—a rehab nurse, Jan's sister and family, the Hispanic neighbors who recently moved in down the street from the Mash's, another family coping with the paralysis of their eighteen-year-old daughter.

By spring of the following year, a regular Bible study and prayer time was meeting every Tuesday night at Richard and Debra's house. The den was full of people who were on fire with life from the other side. It was like being in love again . . . the sky was bluer, sounds more musical, and everyone's eyes had a fine twinkle. Easy and full laughter flowed like a river. Twenty-two people were living in the midst of a "visitation." Some were longtime church members; some had never thought of attending church. Some had a "born again" experience; others didn't know what that meant. Spider was walking again, but barely. And, Debra's face had candlepower; she almost glowed in the dark. Convenience store clerks and waiters routinely asked her why she's so happy. "Come to our house Tuesday night and see!"

When the group gathered, they were amazingly God-focused. They deeply loved, but were not very impressed with, each other; they were fascinated only with God. And, they sought him earnestly, deeply, and lovingly. They would gather in a room, completely comfortable with silence, and just focus on him. Then, His Presence would enter the room and commune with them. They would stand, in deference to present Royalty, and their hearts would swell and a sound would begin to stir. Before long, anthems of worship would roll from those gathered.

Sometimes they wondered if the roof of Richard and Debra's house was trying to get airborne.

And, there was something galvanizing about Richard. His

father's death and his son's long hard road of recovery had beaten the hell out of him. A new man had emerged. People wanted to stand next to him; he was like a campfire on a cold night. His words took on a life-altering vitality. Increasingly, he spoke with humble yet powerful authority. When he opened the scriptures, people leaned in toward him. He began training other men. They met over breakfast, agonized together over family budget crises, and took fishing trips together.

Knowing that he too needed training and personal care, Richard reached out to an enigmatic, but respected, "mystic," a proverbial wise man on the mountain. The relationship was graced by God and brought Richard into increasing maturity as a shepherd.

One Tuesday night in November, just as Richard was preparing to open the scriptures to the little flock, a first time visitor named Ramos asked aloud, "So, what do you call this?"

"Call what? Richard asked.

"This meeting."

"Uh, I don't know," Richard stumbled; he looked around the room. "I guess just getting together with friends."

Others joined in the conversation . . . "I just have 'Mash group' on our household calendar, "Yea, I have 'Prayer Meeting' in my Outlook," "Barb and I just call it 'Tuesday Night Group.'"

Richard explained, "You see, Ramos, we're just a group of friends who get together every week. Our purpose is to reach out for God. But, we're not an organiz –?"

"You're not a church?" Ramos interrupted

"Oh, no, no." The chorus of voices bounced around the room. Warm laughter and the sips of coffee punctuated the moment. The stranger realized he was sitting in the midst of something fresh and real. Richard picked up his Bible and began to read. Once again, expectancy and excitement charged the atmosphere.

Over a period of a few months, as the group expanded, various forces—cultural, psychological, legal—began to stir. The Mash home was getting crowded; they began to talk about the possibility of gathering at a centrally located motel meeting room. They would need a checking account. A neighbor who was a lawyer explained the need for the Tuesday night group to be a tax-exempt, IRS-designated 501 (c) (3) organization. They would need articles of incorporation, a charter, an organizational model.

Obviously, in order to do all that, they needed a name. A wide diversity of suggested names, mainly of Biblical or geographical reference, poured in. Finally, all the fluttering birds settled and began to coo around Psalms 27. The group was born in a great crisis of death and injury. They sought refuge in the Lord. They found his place of safety, the tent (vs. 5) of God. So, it was formally recommended that the legal name be *Tent of God Fellowship*. All documentation was processed and submitted. A bank account was opened. A contract for the meeting space was signed; Richard arranged for a church loan for Tent of God Fellowship to buy musical equipment and a PA system. They—these friends drawn together around God—were now known as Tent of God.

Of course, in time, the fluidity of language turned it from Tent of God Fellowship to Tent-a-God to Tennagod: "We go to Tennagod." "I'm part of the youth band at Tennagod." "Hey, I've seen you folks at Tennagod."

Today, Tennagod has a 25-million dollar campus, a TV show, a magazine, a day care center, an inner city outreach, and a K-8 (soon to be K-12) school. The church website won an award from a Christian web design association. Their logo—the famous blue tent curled about by an orange flame—brands Bibles, coffee cups, computer mouse pads, T-shirts, bumpers, the sacks of groceries and clothing handed out to the poor, and the lower-right corner screen of every video production.

Sadly, Richard began to drift mentally and emotionally after Debra was diagnosed with breast cancer. His sermons lacked something. Glances, confused or ominous, passed between the eyes of old friends. Richard was finally placed on administrative leave by the elders. After Deb's funeral, he wandered for a while, and finally sold the house and got a job in telemarketing. Tennagod hired a new pastor. He's good, the people who loved Richard now love the new guy. He's obviously the future. Everyone is very busy.

But, the river of joy seems to have receded from its old high-water marks. And, no one leans into messages anymore.

I'm not delusional; I don't assume that local churches in America will, or even should, "de-name" and revert back to an unsullied and undefined essence. As Americans, we have the blessed right of free association. So, as long as a group of people are willing to pay the expenses on an institutional entity, that's fine with me. I may even join them.

But, I do think we should at least examine the characteristics of "valley life." Things like marketing, branding, and even the naming issue shouldn't just be embraced without scrutiny. The real question is how much of the atmosphere, the water supply, the social ecology of the valley has infiltrated into the ideas which we assume are Biblical and spiritual?

Understanding that may increase our desire to leave the valley behind and ascend the mountain of Christ.

Chapter 11

MINE EYES HAVE SEEN
THE GLORY

Garrison Keillor walked out on the stage that warm summer evening and told the audience, "Now, we're gonna do a little gospel number for you. If you know it, please sing along." Then, he and the band and singers launched into *His Eye is on the Sparrow*.

I was there that night—Wolf Trap National Park for the Performing Arts in Vienna, Virginia—and what I saw and heard next was a radiant shaft of transcendence. Five thousand Washington, DC people came together in a soulful reach, an astonishing and powerful harmony. . .

I sing because I'm happy.
I sing because I'm free.
For His eye is on the sparrow,
And I know He watches over me.[28]

This was not some little folk ditty or hootenanny sing-along. It was a full-throated choir of groaning strangers. Arms were stretched high in the night air. Eyes were closed. My throat burned and my spine and arms were electric ice.

It was an eternal moment. Very disparate (and surely many *desperate*) people were brought into concert around the Lord. He magnetized the atmosphere, drawing people toward his *Presence*.

---

[28] Words by Civilla D. Martin, public domain

I was overwhelmed at the generosity of God; he didn't seem to are if everyone had "accepted Jesus." Like the rain that falls on the just and the unjust, his kindness didn't pre-qualify anyone. The refreshing shower came on and for dry and thirsty souls.

As I looked around in awe that night, I saw more than the color wheel of ethnicities and clothing; I kept hearing an internal drumming chant, "The promise, the possibilities, the promise, the possibilities…" Being a Washington audience, I knew I was standing in a great human sea of political diversity. None of that mattered. Every earthy thought and sensibility had to bow before an overwhelming Presence. I don't think I'll ever get over what I touched that night.

That evening remains one of the clearest metaphors of the church I've seen. Dissimilar people stepped into an updraft that swept them above the lowlands and onto the higher ground of promise and possibility. No one was planning or searching for it. No one came expecting it. No one deserved it.

A generous God simply chose to drop in and visit some of his people.

Those visitations still (and always will) happen. Sometimes, like the Wolf Trap evening, they are a flash of lightning. They happen once and those present will never meet together in a similar moment again. At other times, he chooses to continue in a time and place for a season.

When the visitations last for a while, we tend to end up calling that encounter a "church." Now, obviously, institutional church patterns have clouded this dynamic. It is no longer necessary for the Spirit to birth anything; a corporate office simply extends a franchise to a new city or neighborhood and begins to measure growth and market share.

But, in a pristine sense, a local church comes into existence when God speaks from his realm and that word crashes into earth. When that happens, people are drawn into concert around God and begin to walk in obedience to his word. And, that concert around him gives birth to a spiritual family; it becomes a home, a haven; it carries echoes of Heaven. But, it does not carry assumptions about leadership, church government, meeting times and places, building programs, or even theology. All of those tend to come much later (usually on the downhill side of the visitation).

In that kind of Heaven-invading-earth phenomenon, you simply cannot *wait* to get together, to open the scriptures, to be taught, and to eat and sing and work and play together. The high-water marks of visitations are those times when he seems to inhabit his people. Another high point of that kind of life is simply running into the other people of the visitation...at the grocery store, a ballgame, or at home gatherings. You love them, not because they're cool or rich or beautiful, but because they carry the scent of God; they were all in the room when the fragrant bottle burst open.

Mine eyes have seen the glory. I have been there. "For one brief shining moment" there was a wondrous and breathtaking visitation, and it included me and my house. 1973—1976, Pascagoula, Mississippi. People who were just strolling along life's seawall were abruptly caught in a from-out-of-nowhere tidal wave.

From my own experience, I know that when that happens, one's only awareness is of that explosive surge, that geyser of Spirit, shooting up from the nearby rocks. You are so drenched and stunned that you're oblivious of everything and everyone on the beach. Self-awareness is stunned and staggered. You're not horny, hungry or thirsty; you're not an American, a Christian, or married. In that moment, everyone is totally overwhelmed by the face and word of God. You don't even know (or care) if you'll survive this encounter.

Over time, as the water recedes, you begin to look around. Dazed, blinking. Everything moves in slow motion. You wonder if you're alive. Then, you feel the familiar touch of your wife and children. Other human shapes and sounds begin floating into your senses. Relationships are formed. A socializing process begins; a local church is born.

Over time, other folks who heard a loud noise come running down to the beach. Even though the waters have receded, they are drawn to a strange essence in the survivors. New friendships are formed; their hearts are joined to yours. The church is growing with a natural and joyful vitality. It is a well-watered and cultivated garden. Life is good.

Later and quite naturally and appropriately, leadership emerges, order is established, theology becomes more of a priority, and conformity takes over. Before too long, they begin to talk about leaving a legacy—things like training the next generation, writing books, and recording albums. In time, the sun moves on and twilight shadows fall across the people.

At the twilight of a visitation, Psalms 74:15 holds a powerful and liberating lesson. It is this: the same God who broke open the fountains of their visitation is the same God who, in his kindness, dries up what everyone thought would be an ever-flowing stream. At that point, the wise know that they can either paw the ground where the water used to come out or they can get very quiet and listen. If they are patient and very still, they just might hear a new spring breaking open.

I will always cherish my memories of that moment in time. Of course, I have no illusions that the tidal wave I experienced was historically unique. Others have told me similar stories. I know about that college dorm revival, the wartime prayer meeting, that sovereign visitation on the golf course.

Nor do I assume that because *my* day of visitation has passed that The Day of Visitation is over. Light moves across the land and different people catch it at different times. So, I don't walk a sad and dusty road; I am not an elegist. I have found a new and fully gratifying place in the Lord (admittedly, a long ways from the Christianity freeway).

And, I rejoice with all those who touch that same eternal essence in new places and in new ways. True knowledge of him always carries an unmistakable bouquet. Even when the people and the context look completely different, that aroma of the knowledge of the Lord reveals a sovereign signature.

Knowing Him

Old maps, especially those of the 16th and 17th centuries, looked like animal hides splotched with coffee spills. In one glance, you could see the whole known world or at least a continent. Although short on detail and accuracy, they gave a pretty good sense of place. By gazing at maps, you could get a view of the earth and where your little desert or mountain range or city fit in the larger scheme.

But, maps are changing. Today, the GPS-based navigation systems in cars and the web-based services like Google Maps and Mapquest give no sense of earth or largeness. Rather, they have reduced the globe down to . . . *me*! Driving with an auto navigation system or working an Internet map is to see myself as the center of everything. The world literally revolves around where I am at any given moment. Driving through Dallas, for example, I can see the web of streets for a few blocks around me and how to get to my destination. But, I am oblivious of the larger context wherein I exist.

The ancient cartographers would have never understood the current narcissism of mapping. I suppose that is inevitable; we live in a self-absorbed age. Today, the story is more about the actor than the play and more about the athlete than the game.

Fittingly and sadly, it is also more about the Christian culture than the Christ. The narcissism of our times has brought us to focus on the landscape nearest ourselves. We are so engrossed with the small screen that we cannot see the larger globe of God. We are ecstatic that Denzel Washington, Anne Rice, and Bono all know Jesus. But, we seem incapable of talking very long or very well about the one these celebrities seem to know. So, we're reduced to spouting inanities like "Oh, don't you just love Jesus?"

Well, we might if you knew how to talk about HIM!

Do you ever notice that when we say we're going to "talk about the Lord," we end up at the center of—and he is peripheral to-the conversation? We just don't seem to know him well enough to have intelligent or even interesting conversations about him. In one sense, we only have a copy of a copy of a copy of a copy of him. So, we just end up saying what others have said others have said others have said others have said about him.

No wonder we'd rather talk about ourselves.

The Spirit of the Age—*the Zeitgeist*—has produced maps which so magnify our own existence and place that we cannot see the larger panorama. Like a human thumb hiding the moon, we're too close to our own private reality to see any magnificence.

The simple but profound truth which hides in plain sight is this: it is all about God. He is the beginning and the end. His word governs his universe. He initiates; his creation responds. Just like the

Wolf Trap evening, he chooses to visit. He magnetizes and draws people to himself. Those moments are entirely borne of his own purposes; they are not conceived or controlled by us.

That means if we're going to know him, we have to clear the decks of every other assumption, consideration, desire, personal preference, and issue. We have to become like a child (knowing nothing) in order to enter the kingdom at all (Luke 18:17).

When Paul said (Philippians 3:8-10) that he considered "all things" to be loss in view of the surpassing value of knowing Christ, did he really mean "all things?" Would "all things" include human concepts about "church?" Furthermore, when he said that he evaluated them as "rubbish" for the same reason, was he serious? ("excrement" is probably a more accurate interpretation than "rubbish." In fact, Eugene Peterson had the scholarly courage to translate it as "dog dung" in *The Message*)

Paul seemed to reveal a fierce, uncompromising, damn-the-torpedoes fixation on getting through, past, around, beyond "all things" and considering them as excrement so that "*I may know Him and the power of His resurrection and the fellowship of His sufferings, being conformed to His death. . .*"

Real Life

I suppose that one way of summarizing the message of this book is…*live*!

History is not off the rails. God is not perplexed or sulking. The tide comes in; the tide goes out. Low tide is as inevitable *and as appropriate* as high tide. When the tide is out, it doesn't mean that God is in a bad mood or that the Antichrist is leaping out of his cage. The tides are simply part of God's rhythmic care for his creation. We just have to learn which activities and ventures are suitable for particular tides and seasons.

The Bible is not about high tide. It's a real book about real life. At the risk of cynicism, I believe that much of the Christian culture roar—"this is a new day…we're just about to see something historic…I truly believe that Jesus is preparing to come back…revival is going to sweep the land like a prairie fire"—is pure marketing. Just the fact that someone's words are carried through the media of television doesn't mean they are delivering a prophesy from God. Our profound silliness about these things is a yard stick of how much we've been pressed into the mold of our times.

Living life straight ahead is always appropriate. While life looks different at low tides, it is still a laboratory and display window for the classic disciplines, graces, and responses. Even in bad times, we can and should trust God, live temperately, love, give, receive, be joyful, be peacemakers, etc.

In every season, God's eyes still search the earth, looking for those whose hearts are completely his. And, when he finds them, he shows them strong support (II Chronicles 16:9). Giving a whole heart to God is appropriate in any season.

Up There!

I've always loved Isaiah 60:1-2 in the New International Version: "Arise, shine, for your light has come, and the glory of the LORD rises upon you…the LORD rises upon you and his glory appears over *you*." (italics mine)

The glory of God always seems to come in *upon* or *over* us. It never seems to pop out of what we're doing; it doesn't boil out of the ground. His glory is like the eagle swooping down over the beetle collector. It is always a surprise.

The next couple of chapters provide an essential tour of the Christian culture. My reason for doing so is not disparagement or voyeurism. Rather, it is to understand the scope of "all things" which may seem essential, but in fact are to be considered as loss and excrement in pursuit of knowing him.

Because of the narcissism of our "maps," very few have any concept of the Lord's enormous kindness, majesty, beauty, thoughts, plans, and generosity toward his own creation and his kids. We've been called beyond, through, around, and over "all things" for the surpassing treasure of knowing him.

I believe God is delivering a new day and a new world—one that doesn't have human fingerprints all over it. So, as you read further, "lift your eyes and look…" A lot of bullshit is washing away. Let it go. Let your eyes see a new glory, a glory that has more to do with the whole earth than it does the provincialism we call "the church."

Chapter 12

THE COST OF PROGRESS

My question that sweet April morning at a bustling city sidewalk café was simple, "From your vantage point, how do you view the church in America?"

The man sitting across the table from me was not only my friend, but a lawyer who has worked many years within the realm of the largest churches and Christian organizations in America. He is also a leader in his local church. His words weigh about three hundred bucks an hour.

He took a long sip of coffee and sat the cup down. He gave the question enough time and then softly and simply replied, "No one cares."

When I asked him to elaborate, he continued, "Too many Christian leaders do not know their people." He paused, and then continued, "During the past thirty years something has changed. Today, most megachurch pastors and Christian organization leaders are entrepreneurs—one who sees a need and fills it. They are not shepherds."

After another sip of coffee, he continued,

"As entrepreneurs, they are primarily concerned with producing growth. It is very important to them for other people to buy into their vision—they evaluate people according to how much they support the program; you know, bigger is better. But, they don't actually care for people."

He went on to describe this growing crisis in the church.

"Too many of today's pastors are simply not shepherds; they don't care about, or even know, their people . . . churches have become so large that it's impossible for leaders to know the people they lead. This is a vicious cycle; they just measure what can be measured — attendance, financial data, program assessments, etc. Most will never invest the time required to know the true spiritual condition of their flock."

Turning Father's House into a Market

A month later, I attended a Sunday morning service in a prominent American megachurch. I sat there, somewhat dazed; at long last, it seemed that the local church had been reduced to a television show: fogging, stage band and singers, digital projection of MTV-like imagery, "smart" sound system, and special lighting for mood management. After the 13.3 minutes of "worship," the "pastor" took the platform. He beamed his smile toward the cameras and talked about how important "each of you are to me." But, clearly, a shepherd was not talking; he was a VP of Sales and Marketing, energizing the team to go out and sell the church. He didn't have care in his eyes or his voice. Those of us assembled before him were only important to the degree that we supported his company.

As we left (exactly one hour after the service started), the foyer had been turned into a store. Books, CDs, sermons, T-shirts, baseball caps, art work, and other merchandise were all professionally presented on display racks and tables. MasterCard, Visa, Discover, Diners Club, and American Express logos were everywhere. Helpful sales representatives greased the flow of products to consumers. The atmosphere was punctuated by the sound of credit card machines.

As I fought my way out of the building, the irony was inescapable. Jesus' words boomed in my head, "*Get these out of here! How dare you turn my Father's house into a market!*"

Of course, you may be thinking, "that's an unimaginative criticism, a very easy target." Exactly! So, how is it even possible that spiritually and theologically mature leaders never collide with those words when *they* walk through it? Does the admittedly easy criticism ever enter *their* mind? Do they, even among themselves, ever submit such practices to serious and honest examination?

The competing views of money—God's and ours—have broken into full and graphic display in the contemporary church with the advent of marketing philosophy and technique.

Marketing is, of course, the science of matching goods (products and services) to needs. As such, it involves the identification of (even if it has to create) consumers and their "needs," the intensifying and rationalizing of consumer desire, and the speedy exchange of money and goods. A market economy is valuable in resisting the centralizing and controlling impulses of government. And, it is demonstrably true that a market-based economy brings higher standards of living wherever it flourishes.

But, that is precisely what makes it so dangerously seductive!

It is such a precarious issue, a true slippery slope. The very thing that makes it such a powerful economic engine is what makes it so improper and malignant for the church—it is a way of viewing the world, a way which sees people, resources, and possibilities in relationship to their profit potential.

Yet, today's church in America increasingly views people through a marketing lens. As such, people are seen primarily as "assets." And the work of business is to do all possible to find, keep, and grow those assets. The "all possible" essentially magnetizes people's spendable money, causing it to almost fly out of pockets or bank accounts or credit capacities and scream through the air, often at warp speed, to become fused to the business interest.

According to Daniel Bell, the three social inventions which cleared the way for consumption to become the driver of economics were:

- Mass production on an assembly line.
- The development of marketing, which rational-ized the art of identifying different kinds of buying groups and whetting consumer appetites.
- The spread of installment buying, which more than any other social device, broke down the oldProtestant fear of debt. [29]

In the years since Bell wrote that, the church has become one of the primary American cornerstones of marketing, consumption, and debt. It seems that the Spirit of the Age discovered and then roared through the church. As a result, we are deluged by an open fire-hydrant of "Christian" books, CDs, movies, magazines, websites, catalogues, cruises, festivals . . . the church is a crucial part of that powerful jet engine of "identifying buying groups and whetting consumer appetites." Churches even encourage parishioners to give offerings through easy credit.

Obviously, the intrusive impact of marketing has transformed the face of the modern American church.

Elmer Towns says that today "American Protestants choose churches on the basis of what affirms us, entertains us, satisfies us or makes us feel good about God and ourselves."[30] That kind of consumerism has pushed local churches from a parish concept to a market-driven one. People no longer go to the church on the

---

[29] Daniel Bell, *The Cultural Contradictions of Capitalism* (New York, Basic Books, 1978) p. 66

[30] Elmer Towns, *An Inside Look at Ten of Today's Most Innovative Churches* (Ventura, CA: Regal Books, 1990), p. 196

corner or the one of their tradition; they drive to find the one that suits their felt needs—worship style, children's program, senior citizens' activities, cell-church structure—most perfectly (just as they would drive to find a Nordstrom, IKEA, or Chili's).

Divide, Isolate, and Confiscate

One of the by-products of marketing is that the idea of progress has become a preeminent value. The pipeline of distribution requires new technologies and ideas in order to remain full of goods and service. Hence, we have a cultural assumption that we must have progress. The ancillary ethos to that assumption is: "we do it because we can" (why else would we manufacture and market battery-powered corkscrews?). Progress is its own validation. As the old General Electric marketing slogan said, "Progress is our most important product."

But, progress always comes at great cost. While marketing has admittedly been and continues to be a major driver of a high standard of living to much of the world, shouldn't it also be examined by the yardstick of what it takes away from us?

British historian Peter Laslett wrote:

> "Every relationship in our world which can be seen to affect our economic life . . . is expected to change of itself, or if it does not, to be changed, made better, by an omnicompetent authority. This makes for a less stable social world . . .
>
> ". . . industrial societies, we may suppose, are far less stable than their predecessors. They lack the extraordinary cohesive influence which familial relationships carry with them, that power of reconciling the frustrated and the discontented by emotional means. Social revolution, meaning an irreversible changing of the pattern of social relationships, never happened in traditional, patriarchal, pre-industrial human society." [31]

---

[31] Peter Laslett, *The World We Have Lost* (New York, Charles Scribner's Sons, 1971) p. 4

It would seem that, among other things, progress has cost us stability, cohesion, and familial and societal rhythm.

Progress is often a thief. The Bible tells the story of a time when Israel's leaders decided to cash in the old-fashioned ways of God for a more progressive approach of a king. They told Samuel to go break the news to God. Of course, God accepted their vote. But, in doing so, he just happened to mention to Samuel how the new progressive way would affect human life:

> "This will be the procedure of the king who will reign over you: *he will take* your sons and place them for himself in his chariots and among his horsemen and they will run before his chariots. . .
>
> . . . *He will also take* your daughters for perfumers and cooks and bakers.
>
> And *he will take* the best of your fields and your vineyards and your olive groves, and give them to his servants.
>
> And *he will take* a tenth of your seed and of your vineyards, and give to his officers and to his servants.
>
> *He will also take* your male servants and your female servants and your best young men and your donkeys, and use them for his work.
>
> *He will take* a tenth of your flocks, and you yourselves will become his servants. (I Samuel 8:11-17 NASB, *italics mine*)

One of the cornerstones of creation is the intimate, sacred, and creative partnership between God and man. The agrarian or sea-faring ways of life are classic representations of that relationship.

So, when progress insists that a factory will produce certain goods faster and cheaper, it is telling the truth. It will admittedly bring a new vitality to the economy. But, there is also a theft going on. The factory will be seizing much of what once belonged to that creative partnership; it will confiscate vast territories once marked by the sweet rhythms of God's blessing on individuals, families, and communities. Part of the sense of disjunction or anomie that we feel today is because progress has so radically compartmentalized and specialized modern life. It has broken life into pieces. And, those shards have been gathered up and confiscated by market forces.

For example, once upon a time, a doctor cared for his patients. What he lacked in medical knowledge was more than matched by the genuine depth of his relationships and concern. He was not only their doctor, but he attended church and ball games with them, came over in the middle of the night if necessary, and even prayed with them. Today, the market forces have compartmentalized and isolated the details of the patient's health and apportioned them out to various specialists, hospital, clinics, laboratories, HMOs or insurance companies, and processes.

Is it purely incidental that each of the compartments is very expensive? Isolation is such a crucial part of progress: it maximizes demand and relinquishes personal control over to monolithic political and economic forces. God created us to live in relationship; we are more than the sum of our parts. When we live in interdependence, we have a mutually beneficial economy. We cooperate in the details of life: gardening, transportation, childcare, even housing. But, isolation means that we have to individually purchase each detail.

Wendell Berry says "The modern urban-industrial society is based on a series of radical disconnections between body and soul, husband and wife, marriage and community, community and the earth . . . Together, these disconnections add up to a condition of critical ill health which we suffer in common . . ." In fact, Berry believes that now "our economy is based on this disease. Its aim is to separate us as far as possible from the sources of life (material, social, and spiritual), to put these sources under the control of corporations and specialized professionals, and to sell them back to us at the highest profit.[32]

Berry brings up another example: breast-feeding. He believes that, after centuries and millenniums, breast-feeding fell out of favor because our economy could not tolerate the free delivery of milk to infants. So, it looked for a way to come between the baby and the breast. The answer was found in undermining confidence in the quality of the mother's milk. The market came up with an "improvement" which it sold in convenient cans.

The same kind of "divide and conquer" tactic can be seen in sexual intimacy. Once it belonged solely and simply to the realm of the mystical union of a man and woman. God designed it and gave it as a gift. But, the market had to find a way to profit from this timeless human drive. So, it intruded into this most private area. First, it promised new freedom and power through the technology of birth control. Then, came the market-driven flood of abortion, pornography, sexual clinicians, erectile dysfunction drugs, and then the staggering medical costs of repairing or alleviating sexually transmitted diseases.

And, yes, all of these areas are enormously profitable.

So, what is the church's response to the disconnections?

Progress seizes the means of production away from individuals, families and communities; it breaks the once seamless ways of life down into disconnected pieces. Then, it employs people and technologies to take over and manufacture those pieces quickly and cheaply, and finally sells them back to us at an attractive profit.

That process disembowels something out of people. It's worse

---

[32] Wendell Berry, *The Art of the Commonplace* (Washington, DC, Shoemaker & Hoard, 2002) p. 132

than a lobotomy. It not only renders people mindless, but ruptures their spirit and spills their capacities for creativity and hard work out on the ground. They end up passive, stupid, and enslaved. Dehumanized.

Berry is right: disconnection is a serious disease. When the parts of the body are disconnected, they die.

What is the church doing in the midst of disconnectedness? Is it repairing "the disconnections?" (Isaiah 58:12) Or, has it fallen in sync with the fragmenting which is part of the industrialization model?

I personally believe that a private home is the best venue for a local church meeting. As the church grows, other homes naturally become centers of church life. A church that gathers in a home remains small, close-knit, organic, and inexpensive. Most important, the parts are connected.

As churches "progress" away from the home to a larger and more institutional structure, a spirit of disconnection takes over. Progress clamps down on and takes ownership of every area in church life. A trend of compartmentalization, specialization, and expense develops.

For example, as soon as a family walks through the front doors of a church building, children, parents, and grandparents are pulled into opposite directions, disconnected locales, and activities "appropriate" to their age and interests. Mirroring the culture, as a local church gets larger, each step of church life gets more conformed to the industrialized model—complicated, fragmented, and managed by "specialists" (most of whom are on salary).

The church jobs program

One of the prime motivations of progress is increased employment. By taking production away from the organic roots (like the family farm) and mechanizing it and moving it into the realm of corporations, jobs are created. Likewise, church progress has created an enormous jobs program, an unbelievable array of jobs.

Today we have the seminary or university trained youth leader, worship leader (or "worship environment facilitator"), children's pastor, missions director, facility manager, counselor, administrator, education director, and on and on. Beyond the local church, a myriad of Para-church ministries have proliferated across the landscape.

For example, at one time churches grew naturally in accordance with patterns of spiritual family. Today, "Church Planter" is increasingly a market-driven job description. A modern church-planter is a religious entrepreneur who identifies spiritual consumers and their needs, awakens and justifies consumer desire, and then unites those consumers with their desires. A church is born.

One church-planting model is based on direct mailing (and/or telemarketing) several thousand people within a tight geographical radius, advertising a new church and giving time and place details. It has been repeatedly proven that a few hundred people will show up for the first meeting; enough of them will continue long enough to fund a pastor and other start-up costs for one year.

Even the role of "Pastor" has become molded by the assumptions of progress. Once upon a time, a pastor knew he was integrally related to the congregation, to serve them with the word, marry and bury them, and, as a shepherd, to lay his life down for his sheep. Relational conflicts had to be worked out; after all, he had to live with those people. Financial shortages had to be taken to the Lord. Community and church crises gave pastors much needed experience; they just had to just grow up.

But, today, the sacred role of pastor is often just another

career choice. Pastors plan their careers as politicians, lawyers, and accountants do.

One of the best descriptions of life in the ministry was offered by Paul:

> *To this very hour we go hungry and thirsty, we are in rags, we are brutally treated, we are homeless. We work hard with our own hands. When we are cursed, we bless; when we are persecuted, we endure it; when we are slandered, we answer kindly. Up to this moment we have become the scum of the earth, the refuse of the world.*
>
> I CORINTHIANS 4: 9-13 NIV

Not too many applicants for those jobs. However, because of the integration of marketing and ministry, that kind of degrading and sacrificial service is no longer necessary or smart. By simply identifying and reaching the right market groups, it is possible (even easy) for one to live very well in the ministry in 21st century America.

Through the magic of marketing, when things get hot, a pastor just announces that he or she "feels led to start a new work." My email carries regular messages from those soliciting prayer and support for starting a new church or ministry. Despite the religious language, these ministry ventures are often escape hatches from the very conditions which Paul identified as normal ministry. One unintended but quite destructive result of this trend is an increasingly immature pastor-class and, worse, a fragmented and fatherless church.

"Worship Leader" is another new description in the church's jobs program (do you think New Testament writers just forgot to identify Jesus' or Paul's "worship leader?"). According to Dr. Towns: "If we recognize church worshipers as consumers, we will recognize church programs as menus . . . Americans go where they feel most comfortable with the style of worship that best reflects their inclinations and temperament.[33]

Although "songwriter" is a relatively old job, consumerism has transformed it. It goes like this: the market has a voracious appetite for new products to consume. Therefore, it demands people who can come up with lyrics and melodies to put into that consumption pipeline. It's no longer enough to just wait for God to take someone through a furnace, boil and broil their guts, and damn-near kill them (after which, they squeeze it out into something like "He Giveth More Mercy" or "How Great Thou Art."[34]

The jobs program is further strengthened by the professional religionists' entrenched fear of the real working world. Many have been so insulated in the religious world that they have no confidence of being able to navigate real world employment. That naturally leads to a continuation of the jobs program.

Let's be clear: this is the "something" that my lawyer friend said has happened in the church in recent years. As he said, "today's church leaders are entrepreneurs, not shepherds."

Jesus, the Great Shepherd, viewed people as holy vessels and profoundly valuable and cherished creatures of Father God. His immeasurable love for His Father caused Him to care for people. After all, His Father "so loved the world that He gave His only begotten son" as the price for their deliverance

---

[33] Elmer Towns, *An Inside Look at Ten of Today's Most Innovative Churches* (Ventura, CA: Regal Books, 1990), p. 196

[34] A few years ago, I toured one of the leading Christian music companies. An entire floor was dedicated to song writing. Day after day, men and women go to their offices and crank out Christian music: worship songs, tunes about Jesus and mama, country, rock, reggae, rap. Then, those songs flow to people on another floor who "pitch" the songs to publishers and producers.

from the Captor. That kind of love can never find anything remotely compatible or acceptable in a marketing model!

Yet, today, many assume that the church and marketing are a God-ordained marriage. The jacket of a church marketing book helpfully explains: "Although the word 'marketing' never appears in the Bible, the Bible is filled with examples of successful marketers: Solomon, Joshua, Nehemiah, and Paul, to name just a few. As you'll see in this book, these dynamic men of God had the ability to identify people's needs and then find the best ways to meet them. Jesus told his followers to do the same . . ."[35]

The church is his body; it should radiate his attitude toward the earth and the people of the earth. Leaders have a grave responsibility to handle people with his attitude and Spirit.

That should scare the hell out of any merchandising impulses. After all, that is what once caused Jesus to throw furniture in the temple.

---

35 George Barna, *A Step-by-Step Guide to Church Marketing* (Ventura, CA, Regal Books, 1992)

Chapter 13

THE GIVER AND
THE GATHERER

God is a Giver. Out of his bottomless generosity, He scatters. Apparently, it's just not within his nature to cluster or hoard.

God is also a River. He flows continuously, yet is never reduced or exhausted. He has no need to conserve. His own nature is generous and his creation reflects his nature. The river of God is always abundant; always full (Psalms 65:9).

Conversely, man is a gatherer, a hoarder.

Much of life is the continuing struggle between these two poles. That struggle finds vivid illustration in the story of the Tower of Babel (Genesis 11:1-9).

Sin City

Adam and Eve's disobedience of their Father God came to tragic fruition in their two sons, Cain and Abel. One day, while working in the field, Cain murdered his innocent brother.

That homicide introduced Cain to the terrifying reality of God's excommunication and simultaneous mercy. God cursed Cain to a life of vagrancy and danger. But, even in that judgment, the Lord cared for Cain and promised to protect him. Sadly, Cain could not receive care on God's terms. Facing the consequences of his sin and divine judgment, he rejected God's care. So, "Cain went out from the Lord's presence . . ." and gave birth to humanity's best and brightest, including the idea of cities.

History's first murderer, overwhelmed by guilt and fear, built the first city.

Over the coming centuries, sin proliferated to such extent that God eventually took his mop and bucket and scrubbed the whole planet clean of the corruptions of sin. However, He brought a righteous remnant of man, Noah and his family, through the flood. Incredibly, all of humanity was reduced to eight people. The future of the planet was riding in that ark.

After the great flood, God told Noah to get out and replenish the earth (is it significant that he said nothing about building cities?). The Creator of the earth was clearly calling Noah into his own attitude and work list. Following the cataclysmic and depopulating flood, God wanted to get life back out in circulation over the earth. True to his nature, He wanted these folks to scatter.

In addition to everything else the flood did, it probably brought a powerful and gushing renaissance of man's submission to God. People quite naturally learn to respect and obey the One Who has the power to cover the world with twenty feet of water.[36] The era that immediately followed the flood must have been a pristine and delightful time on earth. Sin was, to all observance, gone (no one knew that the very people whom God saved were also carriers of the dormant cancer).

However, with the passage of time, man's nature—and its lurking sin virus—began to stir. The post-flood society finally reached a state of cultural sophistication, the flowering of Cain's legacy.

---

[36] Whether the great flood covered the entire planet or just their known world seems to be a minuscule and meaningless issue. How important could it be whether the Australian outback was covered by water or not?

The society had great clarity, power, and pride. They all spoke one language and that unity of speech built a formidable culture.[37]

Eventually, a group of citizens moved out to the land of Shinar. After settling there, under Nimrod's leadership, they started building a city (which would be called Babel). Babel's tower would be the most prominent feature of the city.

Obviously, the city was built in defiance. *We will not scatter; we will put down roots! We will make a name for ourselves.*

The primary motivations which seemed to converge to build Babel (and all cities) were and are: safety, power, and identity. In the building of a city, man seeks to provide—all by himself—the solution for the situation his sin has created. Because of the breach of sin, he rejects the provisions of God and seeks to produce (and amass) simulations of God's care and protection.

Have you noticed that cities always include towers? Whether skyscrapers, monuments, or church spires, the arrogance of man finds inevitable expression in phallic architecture. I don't believe it's completely related to maleness or even sexuality. But, when a society relies on the strength of the flesh, erections inevitably begin rising toward the sky.

Ancient cities were fortifications. They had walls, even motes, designed to protect the citizens. Josephus and other ancient historians have speculated that the Tower of Babel may have been built as a means of escaping rising water (certainly, the great flood would have been dominant in the cultural memory). If so, the project was an audacious announcement that God was a liar, that he surely could not be trusted to keep the promise of the rainbow (Genesis 9:11-16).

---

[37] The capacity or "wiring" for language is innate. Humans quickly learn to navigate their environment and negotiate their personal needs by making sounds and movements. But, as we mature, we cleverly learn to control our environment with language. As Benjamin Disraeli famously observed, "by words, we govern."

In fact, Babel was the antithesis of trust in, and relationship with, Father God. To a large degree, all cities carry that same genetic code. They all capture and coordinate the very best man has to offer in order to achieve essential services. Cities allow man to find facsimiles of security, strength, and identity which are rooted in a distrust of God. The city is a *place* where gifts, skills, wealth and other resources are hoarded. What goes there often dies there. Because the city never releases its bounty to be scattered by the wind, it is reasonable to conclude that cities represent a systemic rejection of God's giving attitude.

When God "came down to see the city and the tower that the men were building," he was undoubtedly focused on scattering them again. There is no indication that he was angry; He was certainly not threatened. Perhaps, as part of his working day, He simply dropped by the earth, surveyed the work site, and gently jerked the thread of common language. That one simple act pulled them back into his purpose of scattering and replenishing. It was probably just one item on his work list for the day.

The Church of Babel

I believe in the biblical and mystical Church. I do believe it is the body of Christ in the earth. And, I believe that God reveals his wisdom through the church (Ephesians 2:10). Some local churches, born in an encounter with the largeness of God, are living that out.

But, the modern institution we call the "church" often has more in common with Babel than it does with Christ. Too many local churches seem related to the same motives that drove the building of Babel: safety, power, and identity.

Today it is culturally assumed that a local church is both a place and a "gathering" or "congregation." It is a geographical spot where people and wealth and gifts and skills are *congregated*. Naturally, the measure of success is directly tied to the size of that gathered mass. Any dispersion of the mass is usually interpreted as "loss" and is the thing most feared by pastors and church accountants.

When God called Abraham, he told him "I will make your name great." (Genesis 12:2). That promise flowed out of God's generous nature; it was part of making Abraham the fountainhead of blessing to "all people" throughout the whole earth and for all time. Conversely, local churches too often reflect the Babylonian impulse to "make a name for ourselves" (Genesis 11:4). That's why local churches become points of identity. Over time, that point of identity can, and usually does, overshadow any sense of identity in the Lord.

The effects of identity are staggering and continuous. Who we are determines what we do, where we go, and whom we follow. The Bible contains no suggestions that people are to find a sense of identity in a local church. Real identity is found only in Father God. I sometimes wonder if it significant that, in an era of diminished fatherhood, many seek identity in the more feminine idea of the "bride" of Christ.

Identity in the Lord means that we follow him wherever he chooses to lead. What does that leadership look like? Well, consider some historical examples.

He led Noah to build an ark, Joseph to save Egyptian civilization, Moses to lead the largest migration in history, Jael to drive a spike through a man's skull, Hosea to marry a whore, and the disciples of Jesus to steal a pony! He didn't ask one of them to found, lead, or join a Bible study, prayer meeting, or "accountability group." They lived life straight ahead, displayed strength, and took action (Daniel 11:32)! [38]

---

[38] There is a vast difference between "taking action" and activity. Many contemporary local churches are cauldrons of activity, but manifest very little true and purposeful action.

Think about it: How would a typical church body in America today respond to the Lord's leadership in any bold and courageous and giving ventures? The very issue of church identity greatly reduces the available "menu" of responses to his leading. It is almost impossible, in the prevalent congregational church model, to simply launch into an adventure in God; there are bills and salaries to pay, programs to execute, and famous preachers and musical artists are under contract for certain performance dates.

Now, I quickly admit that the old top-down, congregational model is breaking apart. And, that convulsion is releasing churches to be more flexible and resourceful in serving "Heaven on earth." For example, many local churches in Houston and all along the Gulf Coast became veritable embassies of Heaven following Hurricane Katrina. They showed entire cities and even government agencies how to mobilize and manage resources for those in need. No one did it better.

But, too often, a sense of identity in a local church inclines "members" toward passivity. The very act of *going to a place* tends to give an illusion of "action." *We went, therefore we acted*. For that and other reasons, most local churches are plainly not serious environments for taking action. They are designed for passive sitting, like a movie theater.

The first evidence of its artificial, man-centered, heart is that the modern local church is largely contained within a user-friendly climate-controlled environment (Wendell Berry says that we forget the degree to which the Bible is an "outdoor" book). Try to imagine Jesus, Samson, David, Abraham, Peter, Deborah, or a guy like Boaz sitting in the pew, or stadium seats, or folding chairs of your church. These were people of action.

Securing land and building a place instantly limits the where, how, and when of the Lord's leadership. And, assigning a name to that place signals a significant transfer of identity. It reveals the drive to "make a name for ourselves."

In addition to being points of identity, many local churches have also become places of safety. They insulate people from the perceived contaminations and threats of society and even from reality, and drive us right back into that Babylonian bunker of common language.

And, of course, local churches are places of power. The sheer concentration of people creates a power base. That's why sales reps flow toward church offices, developers take the pastor to lunch, and why politicians beg for five minutes in the pulpit.

In true conformity to Babel, many churches accumulate and go to great lengths to avoid any kind of scattering. They then find or create supporting theological principles to support the "gathering." For example, I've observed that wealthier churches tend to be more condescending to the poor. They talk about — and use scriptures to support — concepts like self-sufficiency, giving as a way out of poverty, harnessing free-enterprise principles, "boot straps," etc. The implication seems to be: we must protect ("steward") what we've accumulated.

Rain

Several years ago, in the midst of a hot and dry summer, I worked very hard one afternoon to get our lawn watered. I jerked hoses and oscillating sprinklers around the yard, trying to get just the right coverage.

Just as I would be sure I had finally achieved maximum efficiency, I would see water splashing across a twelve-inch band of driveway or sidewalk. So, I'd finesse the hose a little more to avoid wasting any water. After all, things don't grow on asphalt or concrete; it would be stupid to pay for watering it.

A few minutes later, I was upstairs in our home when I heard a great boom of thunder. Very quickly, the rain started. I ran to the window and gazed out over the yard and neighborhood. What I saw was a revelation . . . water poured from the sky onto roofs, streets, driveways, cars, and sidewalks. In an extravagant waste, water was cascading into our cul-de-sac and down our broad and long asphalt driveway.

In that moment, I was almost sure I heard the voice of God thundering over the land, "Ed, I'm not like you."

Leaving the Legacy of Cain

Matthew 5:44-45 records that Jesus said:

> " . . .love your enemies, bless those who curse you, do good to those who hate you, and pray for those who spitefully use you and persecute you, that you may be sons of your Father in heaven; for He makes His sun rise on the evil and on the good, and sends rain on the just and on the unjust."

These are some of the most radical words ever spoken. Jesus was offering deliverance from the legacy of Cain. He invited everyone who would ever hear those words to come up higher, away from the suffocating claustrophobia of sin, and into the fresh, wide-open breezes of the Fatherhood of God. The only way to do it was and is to make a break with that fearful, guilt-ridden, micro managing "let me do it myself" compulsion.

Jesus calls us to get beyond the pinching calculus of "this one is my friend, but that one is my enemy; therefore to survive, I will bless him and curse her." That attitude reflects the cold clammy fear of the fugitive. Living like that is to make our home in the curse of Cain. With these revolutionary words, Jesus says, "It's over; you're free! All you have to do is reverse the cold human logic of love and hate."

Every day of our life, God sends dazzling demonstrations of his generous attitude. He causes sunlight to spill, splash, and surge full and luxuriously across the entire earth. He orders rain to go out and water crops, increase water tables, and clean the atmosphere for *everybody*! Incredibly, He does it without regard for who blesses or curses their Creator. He seems to completely disregard the values or belief systems of the recipients of sunshine and rain.

Sky-filling phenomena like sunrises and sunsets and thunderstorms give us a glimpse of the glorious "pre-Cain" reality. In these stunning daily demonstrations, His Fatherhood calls us up to the higher ground of his generous intentions for life. Paul must have been thinking the same thing when he wrote the words now canonized in Romans 1:20.

> *"For since the creation of the world His invisible attributes, His eternal power and divine nature, have been clearly seen, being understood through what has been made . . ."(NKJV)*

Part of the reason church attendance is declining is that people are tired of the musty, squinting gaze into the dark catacombs of religion. They see more of God on mountain hikes, or sailing ventures, or visits to planetariums, in the pages of the Bible, or in literature and movies. He's everywhere in his creation!

As the "gathering" legacy of Cain (exemplified by marketing and management philosophy) has increased in the contemporary church, Jesus has quietly slipped away from the crowd. Those who keep pawing that old religious ground where the water used to come out are missing the stratospheric, radiant, "giving" glory of his appearance . . . up there!

Chapter 14

THE RIGHT QUESTION

I suppose that minorities in any dominant society—whether racial, religious, economic, moral, physical, whatever—will always be derided, oppressed, injured and even killed. It is a deplorable and yet enduring social evil. It doesn't take long for that complex to cause minority members to react with vengeance.

As a Pentecostal kid, I had a front row seat at the roots of this syndrome. Many of the sermons I heard in the church of my childhood carried themes of "Someday, they'll know and they'll wish they had listened to us." These messages (delivered to people carrying profound senses of inferiority) always projected a vindication too big to miss, a sudden revolving of roles, and a dawning of respect. Preachers talked about folks swimming beside the ark, pounding on the hull, weeping and repenting, begging Noah to let them in. Or, the evil Egyptian soldiers drowning in the Red Sea, wishing they had listened to those pretty-smart-after-all Israelites.

The message was clear: stay focused on what you know to be true and someday "they" will be sorry. Rejection knows how to cook up a kettle of spicy hot revenge. Many fundamentalists I knew not only obsessed about hell, but seemed kinda happy about who was headed that way.

In her fine book on Jewish, Muslim, and Christian fundamentalism, *The Battle for God*, Karen Armstrong details that rejection and revenge syndrome. She wades into the Tim LaHaye territory and examines the attitude of the fundamentalist Christians who . . .

". . . are convinced that suddenly airplanes, cars, and trains will crash, as born-again pilots and drivers are caught up into the air while their vehicles careen out of control. The stock market will plummet, and governments will fall. Those left behind will realize that they are doomed and that the true believers have been right all along. Not only will these unhappy people have to endure the Tribulation, they will know that they are destined for eternal damnation. Premillennialism was a fantasy of revenge; the elect imagined themselves gazing down upon the sufferings of those who had jeered at their beliefs, ignored, ridiculed, and marginalized their faith, and now, too late, realized their error. A popular picture found in homes of many Protestant fundamentalists today shows a man cutting the grass outside his house, gazing in astonishment as his born-again wife is raptured out of an upstairs window. Like many concrete depictions of mythical events, the scene looks a little absurd, but the reality it purports to present is cruel, divisive, and tragic."[39]

I think that vast chasm between the realities of God Who is God and the surreal god we've invented is why the contemporary church is off the rails of history. And, it could be the reason Jesus seems to have disappeared.

Sadly, from the god we've invented, we too often derive a permission, even a command, to abdicate any redemptive, encouraging, and "future-positive" role in the earth. Walk through any Christian bookstore and gaze at the titles, sit in pews in too many American churches, or turn on Christian TV and listen to the static hum of adversarialism toward the world which God so loves.

"*He must punish America or apologize to Sodom and Gomorrah*" must be the most negative, nasty, ignorant, and biblically invalid line anyone has said in recent times.

Years ago, writing about what happened when he took his deteriorating health into his own hands, Norman Cousins deliv-

---

[39] Karen Armstrong, *The Battle for God* (New York: The Ballentine Publishing Group, 2000) p. 139

ered the great summary: "I had a fast-growing conviction that a hospital is no place for a person who is seriously ill.[40] In the same sense, I sometimes wonder if a local church in America is the best place for a person who is trying to follow Jesus.

My personal view is that nothing in the Bible suggests that we are to build, or take responsibility for, the church. The church is his; He said he would build it. I think we need to quit disturbing his land and go find a job in the real world (a.k.a. "the mission field"). Maybe if we did, we would once again see and hear him in the land.

Clearly, "what do we do about the church?" is the wrong question, being asked at the wrong time by the wrong people.

So, what *is* the issue facing us? I believe it is the Kingdom of God.

Thy Kingdom Come

God is the Creator and Owner of everything. That includes every dimension of reality—material, spiritual, physical, ethical, moral, etc. As the Owner, he has designed an order of patterns, laws, and graces for his realm. That order is properly described as the "government" or "kingdom" of God.

Although many centuries of words have been written about the kingdom, we don't seem to be any closer to understanding it. I'm not sure that the kingdom of God can or should be clearly defined or understood. *His path is in the sea; His footprints cannot be traced.* He is The Mystery. *Mysterium Tremendum.* Perhaps we will never come to an "ah ha!" moment where we settle and verify its definition.

---

[40] Norman Cousins, *Anatomy of an Illness As Perceived by the Patient* (New York: W.W. Norton, 1979), p. 29

Apparently, the king himself never did. In the scriptures, we find Jesus saying things like, "Well, it's kinda like seed sown in a field, or it's like a fishing net cast into the sea, or it's like a treasure buried in a field, or it's like a king who gave a party . . ." Not once does this king ever say anything like, "All right people, sit and listen up; I'm going to explain my government and its social vision."

We so desperately want, but never find, that absolute verification. God's eternal truth is, of course, absolute; it is beautifully variegated, multi-dimensional, and transcendent. But, human *interpretation* of truth tends to be too technical, precise, and scientific. Therefore, what often marches under the banner of "absolute truth" may be a fundamentalist reach for the same kind of "science" which they condemn in liberals. And, whether used by conservatives or liberals, scientific or rational methods so often miss him because he is spirit.

Dallas Willard provides a great perception into why we cannot specifically "locate" God or His Kingdom:

> "I occupy my body and its proximate space, but I am not localizable in it or around it. You cannot find me or any of my thoughts, feelings, or character traits in any part of my body. Even I cannot. If you wish to find me, the last thing you should do is open my body to take a look . . . *God relates to space as we do our body.* He occupies and overflows it but cannot be localized in it."[41]

So, we cannot locate or definitively box the kingdom. But, we can say that, in a kingdom, the king makes the rules. The citizens don't. It is not a democracy. Subjects may have personal thoughts about death, justice, the church, sex, bicycles, or bourbon. But, those ideas do not carry force of law. In simple fact, in the Kingdom

---

[41] Dallas Willard, *The Divine Conspiracy* (New York: HarperCollins, 1998) p. 75-76

of God, it doesn't matter what we think. We're citizens of his government. He runs the place; we don't. We have no vote.

God's word and attitude permeate and regulate his Kingdom. And, here's what is amazing: he generously invites those he has chosen to come under the pavilion of his authority and live with him! Those who accept the invitation find themselves "slipping the surly bonds of earth" to rise into his realm. Because his word reigns there, those who have accepted the invitation and embraced his Kingdom find that they are no longer subject to that wretched "inheritance of futility" in the earth (I Peter 1:18).

That's why Abraham was virile and Sarah could conceive a child when they were in their nineties; they dared to believe him and, *like that!*, were free of earthly rules about procreation and parenting. That's why Joshua got a longer day and the disciples of Jesus served healing and deliverance to folks they encountered. They were citizens of heaven walking around on earth. They carried all the rights and authorization of their homeland. More than that, they believed him!

And, that was undoubtedly the backdrop in Jesus' mind when he taught his disciples to pray "Thy Kingdom come, Thy will be done on earth as it is in heaven." He knew the atmosphere and government of Heaven. He was intimately familiar with every nuance of the patterns and rhythms of his father's house. And, while spending time in this captive realm, he probably often groaned those words in prayer.

The captive realm is governed by another kingdom. The Bible calls it the "kingdom of darkness" or "dominion of Satan," etc. That government drives the earth's rampant and intractable conflicts, heartrending cycles of racism and poverty, and the raging inhumanities that defy comprehension. Billions of people are captive citizens of that government. They live under its grinding demands and humiliations. That is why so many go to bed not knowing if they will wake up; why children die of disease, hunger, and exposure; why genocide has cut a destructive swath through the earth for millenniums.

The kingdom of darkness is the death-grip of the old. It is "just the way things are." But, it is dead and has been doing a James Cagney-like slow roll into the dirt for a very long time. The Kingdom of God is the promise; it is the glorious coming down of NEWNESS. The Kingdom is that "new every morning" quality of life.

God has offered freedom and new citizenship to all who want to escape from the degrading government of the old. He welcomes the refugees of that dying realm into the government which is led by Jesus. The swarming, frightened, shell-shocked masses find a homeland that seems too good to be true.

Of course, no one is forced to renounce or migrate from the old totalitarian regime. And, for many reasons, millions haven't or won't. Some don't know about the better land of God's kingdom. Others have heard, but don't believe it exists. Still others just simply do not know how to signal their desire to abandon the collapsing regime. And, as perplexing at it is, some choose to remain under Hell's dominion.

Missing the Point

What role do Christians have in the escape from the old kingdom of Satan's enslavement into the new one of God's eternal promise? Too often, instead of telling people about the new land and government and pointing them a clear escape route, many Christians and churches are caught up in self-promotion or cycles of anger with each other and, worse, hostility toward the captives.

We are sometimes like liberators who arrive in a POW camp which is holding our own fellow citizens. But, rather than working fast to get them out, we waste valuable time building organizations, raising money, and creating PowerPoint presentations which explain again the conditions in the POW camp and the need to leave (dumbfounded looks all around). Furthermore, we make the captives feel stupid and worthless for having been captured in the first place! No wonder so many captives are seriously confused by, or angry at, those strange people who call themselves "Christians."

I can imagine that someday scholars will study the Christian squabbling, reaction, and hostility of our era. I can visualize one of these researchers finally just pushing back from the document table after weeks of study, rubbing the bridge of his nose, and then after a long time of gazing out the window, he turns to the others and says something like,

"Ya know, guys, I don't understand what was going on in those days. It appears that some people who were authorized and equipped to evacuate the captives ended up beating the hell out of each other . . . *and the captives!*"

Too many Christian leaders simply do not understand—or like!—God's purpose in the earth. They are much like Jonah, intensely angry at the measureless panorama of God's kindness and grace.

In the aftermath of Hurricane Katrina, many people were shocked, perplexed, and angry about the mismanaged supply lines—like pallets of bottled water being dropped from such heights that they exploded on impact!—and the atrociously incompetent evacuations from New Orleans.

That may provide a micro-glimpse of the way God views the church's approach to pulling refugees and captives to safety.

Our obsessions with church, hell, the rapture, social issues, etc. are (to borrow Brian McLaren's wonderful phrase) "adventures in missing the point." To focus on the cultural institution which we call the church or the secondary religious issues is like a baseball batter staring intently on the scoreboard rather than the ball.

So, the "right question" is this: are we citizens of His Kingdom? Let's make it simpler than that: are we going to *obey* the King?

The word "obey" cuts to the heart of my independence and rebellion. It is much easier and more insulating to get lost in the rabbit trails of ecclesiology, or corkscrew into the esoterica of theologies, or to attend seminars about "doing church." The maze of church issues allows my nasty self to hide in frantic and breathless activity. Frankly, I think that is why religious people are so focused on church instead of the kingdom.

But, what if we could answer the right question in the right way? Could it be that if we actually focused on—if we would actually *seek*—the Kingdom, then God would add "all these other things (including the church) to us?"

Chapter 15

Walking on the Water

In the darkness of night Jesus made his way down out of the mountain where he had been in conversation with His Father. His three a.m. stroll took him to the shore of the Sea of Galilee. But, when he got to the water's edge he kept on walking. Not only did he walk on water, but he did so through a pitching and rolling sea storm.

Just as this was not the only time he ever climbed a mountain to meet with his father, we have no reason to believe this was the only time he ever went for a walk on the water. And, I doubt that he rode the water like a surfer, arms spread and legs flexed to maintain balance. He most certainly walked in sure-footed confidence, perhaps even unaware that he had left land and crossed over onto water.

Apparently, like his father, the son's ". . . way is in the sea, his paths are in the great waters, and his footsteps are not known."[42] And, also like his father, "night and day, darkness and light, they're all the same . . ."[43] Jesus is not only the king of the created order, but he was the project foreman over building the universe.[44] So, he probably designed and built water itself (a detail which never shows up in his biographies).

We tend to get so focused on the presumed purpose of his late night walk (rescuing his disciples and, by projection, us!), that

---

[42] Psalms 77:19
[43] Psalms 139:12
[44] Hebrews 1:2

we often miss this extraordinary glimpse of his masterful posture toward the creation. Darkness or light, water or ground, storm or stillness, past or present—he strolls through it all without stumbling or wobbling.

The Power of His Word

How do mortals relate to the strange otherness of the one who walks around on water in the middle of a stormy night? He is clearly not like us. In our attempts to shrink and domesticate and control him, we lose sight of the panoramic scope of his largeness.

Ironically, it was a man of very earthy nature, the impulsive and reckless Peter, who stepped into a beautiful revelation that night. His attention zoomed right past the boat and the others in the boat. I can imagine him standing straight up in the boat, face pelted by the horizontal blasts of water, and gazing spellbound at this Man walking through the angry sea. Then, he screams over the howling wind, "If that is you, command me to come to you on the water!"

Jesus is the king of all creation. He built it, owns it, loves it, manages it, and "upholds it all by the word of His power" (Hebrews 1:3). So, Peter quickly cut to the chase. He knew the operative power and only relevant issue was Jesus' spoken word: "*command me to come . . .*" And, sure enough, when mortal man stepped under the pavilion of Heavenly authority, he rose beyond the limitations of earth.

We read it and yet miss it. His word is the power of his reign. He creates by his spoken word and he upholds all things (including a flawed man leaving the security of the boat) by the same potency. When we obey, we step out into the secure grip of God. When we disobey, we sink through the surface of circumstances.

Footprints in the Sea

The way of a ship in the sea

There are three things which are too wonderful for me, yes, four which I do not understand: The way of an eagle in the air, the way of a serpent on a rock, the way of a ship in the midst of the sea, and the way of a man with a virgin.

PROVERBS 30:18-19 NKJV

If Solomon—true wise man—did not understand these four mysterious transactions, then I seriously doubt that I can provide much illumination here. But, I do know that all four of these relationships are genuinely beautiful and spellbinding. And, all seem to illustrate great and wondrous actions which leave no traceable or verifiable evidence (like the footprints of God).

But, the ship in the sea is quite distinct from the others. Of the four objects, it is the only one which is invented by man rather than created by God. Ships, however, are more than just fabricated; they are not at all in the same category as anvils, earrings, or ball bats. In a very unusual way, sailing vessels capture the traces and touches of the relationship between heaven and earth. They are made of earth stuff, but surely inspired by the great Shipbuilder. Noah would have drowned (and every living creature with him) before ever thinking of building a ship. That ship, the ark, was God's idea. And it is easy, when one boards a ship, to sense the Creator in the design and the sailing experience.

Ships offer a security in, and means of travel through, the sea. Like other invented objects, ships find their purpose only in the midst of God's creation. In the Bible, they served not only Noah, but many others, including Solomon, Paul, the disciples, and Jesus. By adding Jonah to the list, we quickly see the problem with ships. They are controllable and, therefore, offer escape from the one who is not. We would all rather deal with a ship than with water.

A ship is such a contradiction; it calls us to adventure and danger, yet also speaks to our need for safety and security.

The church is a ship. It sails and finds its purpose only in the midst of the scary mystery of water. We cannot become settled and comfortable in the ship without losing touch with the mystery. That's why Peter will always remain a timeless and appealing image for us; we're all so necessarily boat-bound, yet we strain for the one who walks on the water. When faith allows us to hear the alternate promise of his spoken word, we gain the confidence to forsake the traditional and manageable securities.

The water always calls out to us. Jimmy Buffett paints it so clearly:

> *Mother, mother ocean, I have heard you call,*
> *Wanted to sail upon your waters*
> *since I was three feet tall.*
> *You've seen it all, you've seen it all.*
> *Watched the men who rode you,*
> *Switch from sails to steam.*
> *And in your belly you hold the treasure*
> *that few have ever seen, most of them dreams,*
> *Most of them dreams.* [45]

The beautiful and terrifying majesty of the ocean embodies the simultaneous terror and invitation of God. Just as he did to Peter, he calls us out of the ship into the greater security of his word.

To never step out of the ship is to become hopelessly and fatally traditional. It is to lose sight of greater (and, yes, more threatening) possibilities. The saddest sailor is the one who dropped below deck, became ensconced in an invented and preferred environment, and never emerged to gaze at the sea again.

---

[45] Jimmy Buffett, *A Pirate Looks at 40* (Copyright 1974, Jimmy Buffett)

What Should We *Do*?

At this point, you may be earnestly wondering, so what do I do about this? And, as I wrote on the first page, that is the wrong question. The fact that we even think in terms of "do" reveals our confusion.

If you think of faith as our relationship to water, you quickly see that most of our "do" questions are boat related.

"What does a New Testament boat look like?"

"Should brothers and sisters ever be asked to leave the boat?"

"How should we 'do boat' in a postmodern era?"

"Where are the blueprints for the boat?"

"How do we resolve boat conflicts?"

As such, they reveal our estrangement from a natural world and our investment in a manufactured environment. Once, people thought and spoke in the language of the land or sea, seasons, and the cycles of birth and life. Today we speak of "principles for success." (Am I the only one who finds "principles" to be sterile, suffocating, and boring as hell?)

We've traded organic perspectives and assumptions, such as agrarian, nautical, or meteorological ones, for the invented paradigms of business, marketing, technology, time management, etc. This is much more than just a simple choice of word pictures. The natural order carries a greater awareness of dependence on God. The world we have made is shaped by human capacities and control. Big difference.

Martin Luther said, "The sin underneath all our sins is the lie of the serpent that we cannot trust the love and grace of Christ and that we must take matters into our own hands." At the risk of simplicity, I think the real and only question is: "Do I trust God?" All of life tends to boil down to that one question.

That's why the way we think about God is so crucial. When we see him as the CEO, a marketer, a time management expert, or a therapist, then we move him into constructs which permit more human competence and control; we can now approach him through a matrix that we designed. But, the natural order is so mysterious—who can understand a seed, a hurricane, or the life arc of the cicada?—that it seems to lock us out of any "partnership" with him, at least on our terms.

In the course of my consulting, the head of a Christian ministry once spoke to me at length about his requirement that "we (himself and his staff) must grow this ministry." By that, of course, he meant that he wanted to increase the spiritual, financial, and market strength of his organization. Understandable. But, his statement revealed a grotesque monster; that enormous and arrogant sense of independence which has now become an unquestioned assumption throughout modern Christian-think. Our personal sense of "do" has eclipsed our submission to, reliance on, and gratitude for God. We've been so invaded by management philosophies and marketing strategies that we've become unhooked from the mother ship. We're floating off into space; our oxygen is running out and we don't even know it.

Growth is a mystery, a phenomenon that is both natural and supernatural. It is neither a function nor the result of management.

For example, sperm can be received or it can be analyzed. If it is received, it does its invisible and inscrutable work; new life springs from the womb. However, if it is caught in a cup and taken to the laboratory so that we can break it down, subject it to catalytic agents, and study it, the sperm dies. Life and growth belong to him.

Consider how Jesus described the mystery of growth:

. . . A man scatters seed on the ground. Night and day, whether he sleeps or gets up, the seed sprouts and grows, though he does not know how. All by itself the soil produces grain . . .

(MARK 4:26-27 NIV).

And, James offered a consummate correction to the "We must grow it" mentality when he wrote:

Now listen, you who say, "Today or tomorrow we will go to this or that city, spend a year there, carry on business and make money." Why, you do not even know what will happen tomorrow. What is your life? You are a mist that appears for a little while and then vanishes. Instead, you ought to say, "If it is the Lord's will, we will live and do this or that."

(JAMES 4:13-15 NIV)

One yardstick of our deception about the nature of growth is the syncretism of faith and business. It is a dangerous illusion to assume that ministry operates by the rules and reasons of business. Business is about success and continuity. Ministry is about life poured out. "Success" in ministry brings us into a personal embrace and embodiment of the death of Jesus.

The real issue is relationship, not "do."

When we trust him and his word, we are grafted into his body. At that point, God—the head—determines what we—the members—*do.* He is the vine; we are the branches.

For example, my hand doesn't have to understand or agree

Walking on the Water   **157** with the mission that I assign to it. ("Now, Ed, I will only do stuff for you in the church.").

Think about it; you send your hands on various missions—dangerous, disgusting, or delightful—and the hands just do what you initiate. Sometimes they get hurt, muddy, or even broken in the work. Naturally, you're always quick to cleanse, repair, and restore them back to their original condition. You "pastor" your hands, exercising great care to protect them, keep them clean and healthy, and make sure they get rest and proper attention. You love them; you and your hands have a great relationship.

I bet you've never had a hand argue with you or quit working while it processed through its self-analysis issues. Have you ever seen a hand just go do something because it was restless, frightened, or bored? Have your hands ever threatened to leave and go join another body?

Much of our confusion about "what to do" grows out of our silly view of bodies and how they work. The question is rarely "can they do it?" The issue is: did you actually direct them to do it?

I believe the normal functioning body is the first guideline governing our "do." The head decides; the rest of the body responds. That clears up a lot of goofiness about "doing church." First things first.

NOTICE: This Book Has No "Takeaway"

Many publishers and readers want books to end with an action list. You know: we're very busy. Yeah, we read the book. We liked or agreed with that, didn't care much for this. Nice story. Good principles. Now, just give me a list that I can *do*.

I hate the term "takeaway." It basically declares that we don't have the patience for process. We do not trust or have time for the "long obedience in the same direction" through which the Lord's nature slowly replaces our own. Just tell me what to do. I can handle it.

But, the fact that we even think that way is the problem. We do not know the quiet and contemplative posture of just sitting at the Lord's feet. We do not realize that the essence of walking with the Lord is osmosis. His spirit just gradually and very slowly seeps into our life. As it does, it takes over. We begin to die and he begins to live through us.

I am not going to wrap this book up with a "do list". . .you know, work in a soup kitchen, volunteer at a hospital, minister to those in jail, clean toxic dumps and roadways. All of those are good.

God is creative; he hands out his own "do list" (and his assignments that are rarely found in manuals). His "do" will always bear his unique signature of creativity and purpose.

Is it possible that our only role is to receive?

The most important thing we can do is simply to receive. Receive him, his word, his majesty, his plans, his power.

Most of us are so attentive and diligent as disciples of this age, that we are firmly integrated—body and soul—into the aggressive taking of what we want. Consumerism, goal-orientation, salesmanship, and old fashioned American ingenuity have converged to form an ethic which eclipses and disputes the biblical idea of "receiving."

One morning, a strange phrase dropped into my mind: "Whiskey in a barrel." I wondered if the Lord was speaking to me. Did he want me to read about it or drink it?

After laboring in prayer, I decided to study it instead of drinking it. Or, at least, *before* drinking it.

I learned that whiskey has to wait a long time in the dark for "the complex interaction" of time and air and oak and "spirit." It takes years of sitting in the dark (Chivas Regal, Dewar's, and others are known for their "12 year" scotch). In the same way, God makes us wait through the very same, very long complex interaction with the same kind of agents.

I don't know about you, but it is very difficult to just give myself to processes which I do not control. An illusion always creeps into the waiting—God is waiting for me to do something, he's waiting for me to wake up, wise up, repent, get a grip, be more disciplined, fast for 40 days, pray without ceasing, go to church. DO something.

Shortly after my whiskey study, I talked to my pastor, Glen Roachelle, about a difficult and immobilizing situation. After listening to my complaint, Glen simply said, "What you've done or not done is not the reason for your place; it's none of your business what God is doing in you."

Yes. The waiting itself is the point. Just as it takes time for "the complex interaction" of distilling spirits, time itself refines and distills whatever God has put into our vessel. Not a thing I can do about it. I can only submit, and die in, the process.

Is that why Psalm 37 says that "the humble" will inherit the land and delight themselves in His abundance? Maybe it's only those who have nothing left—no strength, no good ideas, no connections, no hit songs, nothing of value at all in their own flesh—who are able to inherit the land.

I don't believe that life should be passive. But, our driving passion—our "knock, knock, knockin' on heaven's door"[46]—

---

[46] Bob Dylan, *Knockin on Heaven's Door* (Copyright 1973, Bob Dylan)

should be for his reign in our lives and throughout our environment. That's it.

The legacy of Cain has more of a grip on us than we realize. He could not receive divine protection and provision on God's terms; he had to control the process and the outcome. So, as described earlier, he built a city. In the building of that city, Cain sought to provide his own solution for the problem created by his sin. The city was his self-designed reach for—a taking of—safety, power, and identity.

But, there is a city that God designed, inhabits, and provides. The "New Jerusalem" of Revelation 21-22 embodies all the resplendent abundance which is God himself. At last, he is entirely enough.

In the "newness" which he gives, our only role is to receive. We bring nothing to the process or the outcome. The overwhelming reality of the brand new world in the morning, New Jerusalem, is that he himself dwells there and is everything—even the sun and the moon—which the city needs.

Do we understand that there is no temple in that new City? "The Lord God, the Almighty, and the Lamb, are its temple." (Revelation 21:22)

New World in the Morning

Receiving his newness and entirely sufficient abundance is the primary "do" of our life. The radiance of possibilities, the dawning of a new world, the coming down here of "up there"—these should be the waking fervor of life. The mildewed, rotting, stench of our best efforts—preserving oldness—is the death rattle of all that is abhorrent to the new.

"And He who sits on the throne said, 'Behold, I am making all things new.'" (Revelation 21:5 NASB).

Walter Brueggemann wrote, "The gospel is about the coming of newness into our situation. It has been so since our mother Sarah got the word that she would have a child . . . And news of pregnancy always means a radical change in perception, whether it is the long-awaited, welcome news, or confirmation of one's worst fears. It was newness that night our fathers and mothers left Egypt . . . And it was so every time Jesus came into the life of a person or a community. Wherever he was and to whomever he spoke and whomever he touched, things were new. That's what Jesus is like and what the gospel is about."

"The world does not believe in newness. It believes that things must remain as they are. And, for those of us who are well-off, it is a deep hope that things will remain as they are. Every new emergent is quickly domesticated; and if it cannot be domesticated, it is outlawed or crushed."

". . . The faith community, synagogue and church, exists precisely to announce the new, to affirm that we do not live by what is, but by what is promised."[47]

Because so much of the contemporary visible church has become an agent of the old order, because it is so heavily invested in keeping things the way they are, it has become the direct opposite of the newness that Jesus is and that he brings.

He is not there; he has disappeared.

But, when we—those who try to follow Jesus—divest ourselves from the investments in the claustrophobic old and when we begin to pulsate with the promises and possibilities, then we receive all that he is.

It is at that point that we become heralds of a breaking dawn.

---

[47] Walter Brueggemann, *Peace* (St. Louis, MO; Chalice Press, 2001) p. 131-132

Footprints in the Sea

Life is a continual progression of being squeezed out of small places into larger ones. In birth, we were all rejected by our perfect, climate-controlled, and well-nourished zone of maternal comfort. Then, we were nearly squeezed to death in the birth canal. Had we been wired for language at that moment, we would have surely cried out for God to save us from that claustrophobic death matrix. And then, in an explosion of blood and water, we burst into the infinitely larger place of "real life."

Ah, we sighed . . . now, this is my destiny! Mother's warm breasts, a family to serve every possible need and desire, and the emerging sounds and colors and touches that were unknown in the old, dark, and very cramped world.

However, after a few short years of this "heaven on earth" familial environment, Mom and Dad kicked us out of the nest and sent us to school. There we discovered reading, social interaction (girls! boys!), and playground skills and thrills. We could never go back to the way it was; our destiny had taken us beyond the small borders of infancy.

That process continues, of course, on through the various levels of education, courtship, career, family. We keep filling up spaces, being rejected by them, and bursting into new realms.

Finally, we come to the end of life on this earth. Our spirit can no longer tolerate the suffocating constrictions of earthbound life (I think at the end of life on earth, our spirit knows this is what "old" means; it yearns for newness). The fearful flesh part of our *old* self tries to delay the process. We want to stay in our earth-womb; we want to preserve the old order. Of course, we think of a million good reasons to stop the process. Wait; I want to see the Great Wall of China, meet the Pope, see The Rolling Stones in concert, lead people to Christ, touch my great-great-grandchildren.

But, no. Our environment is kicking us out . . . again. And, a new world in the morning waits.

Is it possible that those who were rejected by the age and squeezed into "the church" are now being pushed through the birth canal . . . again? Are we being squeezed into the larger and newer place of the Kingdom of God? Could it be that those who follow Christ have been in a long and narrow tunnel of "church" existence where we needed the invented light?

But, now perhaps, we're coming out into a new, larger, and surpassing reality.

Are those destined to follow the Christ being squeezed out of the cocoon of all that is old and manageable? Are we being pressed into the larger and "new every morning" dominion of the Kingdom of God? It does seem that the old "boat" is becoming crowded; temperatures and tempers are rising and we're being squeezed out onto the sea.

And, there he walks.

His path is through the mighty and sometimes dark rolling sea. A small splash, a swirl of bottom sand and silt. He's always gone from what we know and understand; he's always walking into the new world of his promise.

He went thataway . . .

I believe Jesus has disappeared from all that is old, including much of American Christianity. Many will ask how is it possible that he has disappeared; throughout the Bible, a promise declares that God will always be with us.[48] He does not forsake us.

---

[48] Genesis 28:15, Deuteronomy 31:6-8, Joshua 1:5, I Chronicles 28:20, Matthews 28:20, Hebrews 13:5 and other scriptures.

But, his promise does not mean that he will show up in the holy places we presume to build. He created the earth and pronounced it "good." Furthermore, the whole earth is (not "will be") full of his glory. What he built is entirely sufficient and "holy." It does not need our revisions, additions, or remodeling.

Yet, for some reason, we keep building 'em. The religious mind will always try to improve on what he speaks and creates. And, the very act of building seems to carry an expectation of "Oh, come on God, you know how much trouble and expense we went to in building this thing. Besides, so many are expecting you to be there . . . so, we're going to announce the weekly times of your appearance . . . OK?"

We keep building boats—religious fishing boats, speedboats, cabin cruisers, schooners, whatever—and expecting him to ride with us. But, he went thataway. He left the boat a long time ago; he's been out on the stormy water for several years. If we want to be with him, we will have to leave our manufactured securities and walk to him.

I do not mean that everyone should leave the church. How many times must I repeat it? How many different ways should I say it?

I do not mean that everyone should leave the church.

I do not think that everyone should leave the church.

I do not believe that everyone should leave the church.

I have never said and will never say that everyone should leave the church.

But, some kind of radical reorienting action may be necessary in order to find the newness of his word and authority. For some, that action may involve leaving the social construct which we call "the church." Others can walk away from a false security without any physical movement at all. Tradition doesn't contradict faith; traditionalism does.

Dietrich Bonhoeffer wrote, "Faith can no longer mean sitting still and waiting—they must rise and follow him. The call frees them from all earthly ties and binds them to Jesus Christ alone. They must burn their boats and plunge into absolute insecurity in order to learn the demand and gift of Christ . . .

" . . . The new situation must be created, in which it is possible to believe on Jesus as God incarnate; that is the impossible situation in which everything is staked solely on the word of Jesus. Peter had to leave the ship and risk his life on the sea, in order to learn both his own weakness and the almighty power of his Lord. If Peter had not taken the risk, he would never have learnt the meaning of faith. Before he can believe, the utterly impossible and ethically irresponsible situation on the waves of the sea must be displayed. The road to faith passes through obedience to the call of Jesus. Unless a definite step is demanded, the call vanishes into thin air, and if men imagine that they can follow Jesus without taking this step, they are deluding themselves like fanatics."[49]

The age of the boat is over. The new era of the water is here.

---

[49] Dietrich Bonhoeffer, *The Cost of Discipleship* (New York: Simon & Schuster, Touchstone Edition, 1995) p. 62-63

Index Cloud

Abraham & Sarah

Agriculture & agrarian life

Babel

George Barna

Wendell Berry

Christianity & Christian Culture

Church:
Universal – Local
Eternal – Cultural
Buildings – Programs
Jobs – Planting
Names
Counterculture

Walter Brueggemann

Chinn:
Amy – Carl – Ed
Eddie – Jack
Joanne – Mary
Paul – Vernon

Cain

Cities

Disconnection

Economics

Faith

Consumerism

Jacques Ellul

God

Goldsberry

Great Depression

Fatherhood

The Flood

Heaven

Hell

Jesus

Kingdom of God

Leadership

Brian McLaren

Mary & Joseph

Marketing

Mosaic Law

Mystery

Paul

Pascagoula, Mississippi

Pentecostal Holiness Church

Pentecostalism

Peter

Eugene Peterson

Pratt County, Kansas

USS Princeton

Progress

Prophecy & Prophetic

Reality

Rain

Receive

Religion

Glen Roachelle

Rock Island Railroad

Samuel

Sensuality

Ships & Boats

Simeon & Anna

Charles Simpson

Solomon – Solomon's Temple

Southwestern Bible School

Charles Spurgeon

Elmer Towns

Tradition

Visitation

Waiting for God

Wealth & Poverty

World War II

Wolf Trap & Garrison Keillor

Worship

Worship Industry

"Once upon a time books were written to be read. Today, they're written to be sold."
Cool River Pub. Books worth reading.

Cool River Pub is a publishing company and a website.

But, as the name suggests, it is also a place to escape the heat, cold and cruelties of life. People need a place of refuge; all are invited to come on in and shake off the harshness which afflicts body and soul in our times.

So, grab a bottle or mug and find the warmth of good friends and honest conversation.

Cool River Pub is a safe place. Those who gather here—authors, readers, listeners, bloggers—are invited to build relationships and share ideas, impulses, and inspirations. And, the house rules invite (and require) good humor, respect, and largeness of spirit.

As a brand, Cool River favors and supports non-traditional and non-religious excursions into the largeness of God and His creation.

Watch Cool River. New books will soon be floating into view.

Let us know how you feel about *Footprints in the Sea* or anything else on your mind. Contact us at brewer@coolriverpub.net.

COOL
RIVER
(PUB

WWW.COOLRIVERPUB.NET